HAS YOUR ROBE BEEN WASHED?

D. L. TREXLER

Has Your Robe Been Washed?

A STUDY OF
REVELATION

PAST

PRESENT

FUTURE

Tate Publishing & *Enterprises*

Has Your Robe Been Washed?
Copyright © 2010 by D. L. Trexler. All rights reserved.

No part of this publication may be reproduced, stored in a retrieval system or transmitted in any way by any means, electronic, mechanical, photocopy, recording or otherwise without the prior permission of the author except as provided by USA copyright law.

Scripture quotations marked (NRSV) are from *New Revised Standard Version Bible*, copyright © 1989 National Council of the Churches of Christ in the United States of America. Used by permission. All rights reserved.

Scripture quotations marked (NIV) are taken from the *Holy Bible, New International Version®*. NIV®. Copyright© 1973, 1978, 1984 by International Bible Society. Used by permission of Zondervan. All rights reserved.

The opinions expressed by the author are not necessarily those of Tate Publishing, LLC.

Published by Tate Publishing & Enterprises, LLC
127 E. Trade Center Terrace | Mustang, Oklahoma 73064 USA
1.888.361.9473 | www.tatepublishing.com

Tate Publishing is committed to excellence in the publishing industry. The company reflects the philosophy established by the founders, based on Psalm 68:11,
"The Lord gave the word and great was the company of those who published it."

Book design copyright © 2010 by Tate Publishing, LLC. All rights reserved.
Cover design by Lauran Levy
Interior design by Christina Hicks

Published in the United States of America

ISBN: 978-1-61739-546-8
1. Religion / Biblical Studies / Prophecy
2. Religion / Christian Life / Spiritual Growth
11.01.17

Dedication

To my father, Rev. Floyd Columbus Trexler, for introducing the book of Revelation and showing me what it means to have, "One's robe washed in the blood of the Lamb."

To my lovely wife, Sandra, for putting up with me as I battled the Beasts from the earth and the sea.

And finally to my home congregation, Gloria Dei (Glory to God) Church in Highland, Indiana, for attending the many classes as I tried to make sense of this glorious vision and for giving me the time to finish what I started.

Table of Contents

Introduction	9
Note to Readers	17
Background on Revelation	23
What Does Revelation Mean?	25
Who Is The Author?	31
Who Is John?	35
Who Are the Seven Churches?	39
Who Are the Twenty-four Elders and the Lamb?	61
What Are the Seven Seals?	71
How does God Warn?	89
Who Are the Characters of Good and Evil?	113
Where Do the Forces of Good and Evil Collide?	123
What Are the Seven Plagues?	141
Who Is the Whore of Babylon?	149
Who Is the Bride of the Lamb?	163
How Does It All End: Hell and Destruction?	167
How Does It All End: Heaven and Salvation?	181
Conclusion	185

Introduction

The story begins in the foothills of the Appalachian Mountains with a blue-eyed, blond-headed, freckled-faced youngster, who by fate or design, was born into the household of a Lutheran Minister—a minister who just so happened to work actively with the civil rights movement in a time and place when many thought too highly of themselves. In the summer of 1966, the boy's father brought an African American professor from one of the local universities to church in that small self-righteous town. The following Sunday, a large sign stood in front of the church, a sign someone had gone through quite a bit of time and effort to prepare, that read, "No Niggers Allowed." This young fellow had never seen his dad so angry. The Lutheran pastor pulled the sign from the ground, broke it over the back pew, and screamed, "Get out! Everybody get out and go home!" As the people filed out of the church, many approached the pastor saying, "We had nothing to do with placing the sign."

To this, the minister replied, "Maybe, but you walked right by it and did nothing."

Canceling church did not sit well with the good Christians of the community. The fine town folk went so far as to bring the ten-year-old's dad up on charges. The brave citizens never did have the gumption to accuse the pastor of their real fears, those of prejudice and total ignorance. Instead, they accused him of playing his ukulele in the pulpit and having a son that ran wild. Now the boy was not really wild, just a little mischievous.

One particular morning, the trial for his father was ending. The rambunctious little fellow carefully filled ten balloons with red carpet dye and water. He shimmied up the gutter to the flat rooftop of the church. When the leading citizens, the chief of police, the furniture tycoons, even the mayor left the room of lies, this not-really-wild-child tossed the carpet dye balloons on them and their cars. Holy cow dung hit the fan! Not only were the town hypocrites livid, the boy's father was fit to be tied. However, I somehow suspect he wasn't as mad as he made out to be. He might have even been a little proud. But that's not the point. The point is the father handed down a serious punishment to this miniature hell rouser. The innocent tyke would be grounded for two long months. Worse yet, he had to read the entire book of Revelation and, to top it off, write a five-page report on what he learned. The little freckle-faced kid suffered through his grounding and nightmares like a man. He read Revelation and wrote that five-page report even though he had no clue as to what he had read. He could not get past all the bizarre symbolism with its seven and ten-headed beasts. Little did the innocent blond-headed, blue-eyed, freckle-faced child of God realize he was actually living in the midst of this fascinating drama called Revelation!

They claim time heals all wounds. Yet I never could figure out who "they" were because, from this young boy's experience, the wounds kept getting larger and opening more deeply. Of course, the minister was found innocent and lovely townspeople guilty, but the injustice and violence would continue throughout the youth's life. The freckle-faced adolescent then moved to Jacksonville, North Carolina, at the height of the Vietnam conflict, a war that lasted too long and accomplished little, where church members were pronounced dead or missing at Sunday services and body bags were seen arriving daily at Camp Lejeune. Later, the youthful soul would pack up and move again, this time to the inner city of Louisville, Kentucky, where he experienced inbred hatred by attending an all African American school with blond hair and bright blue eyes. Here he would physically feel the ignorance of humanity with parents throwing bricks at school buses carrying innocent children simply because of the color of their skin. Yes, this poor confused lad had witnessed firsthand the riders of the Apocalypse at a very young age and didn't even know it.

Time heals all wounds? Baloney! Time made the little, mischievous, lad cold and hard. If anyone asked what he wanted to do when he grew up, he would say, "I don't know, but there is one thing I know I don't want to do, and that is be a pastor!" So for the next thirty-five years, this child of God lived life for himself, always seeking to rise up in the ranks of society, trying to be a lot like the people who had persecuted his father many years ago. After all, if you're not on top, you get squashed. Yet through the years of successfully striving for the material things life has to offer, something happened to this damaged young man. He got married and had children of his own. His father died. He was told he was going to die of cancer, and he battled the beast of alcoholism. Now for some strange reason the meaning and purpose of his existence took on a whole new dimension, but what dimension? This confused, not so young, not so blond man had a dilemma, a dilemma we all face sometime in our brief, unproductive lives. What is my purpose? Why am I here? So by design or chance the still blue-eyed, still freckled-faced man did something he promised he would never do. He left his 4,500-square-foot home, got rid of his boat, sold his Corvette, moved in with his "out-laws," and enrolled at The University of Chicago to become a pastor. Life sure has its share of twists and turns!

Most have figured out by now I am the little mischievous, confused, blond-haired, blue-eyed boy from 1966. When enrolled at seminary, one of the first classes required was entitled "Methods." It is simply a course on *how* to read the Bible. One examines the boring stuff, such as historical background, the setting, the audience, and many other factors trying to arrive at a meaning for now and then. Take one remote guess what book we used as a case study. That's right, Revelation! The honorable Dr. David Rhodes was the professor, and this man, believe it or not, had memorized the entire book of Revelation. Try that in your spare time. Professor Rhodes started out the day "performing" each and every chapter of this odd book. I became fascinated with the message of Revelation, so much so that one could say I became addicted, which is part of my personality. I read these writings of a man named John over and over again, some one hundred times, and listened to the voice tape of the book another hundred. I purchased about every commentary written on Revelation, trying to make sense of a book many claim made no sense. Each time I read or listened to Revelation, I gained a little insight. Each time I read a new commentary, I would pick up bits and pieces of information, but for the most part, I felt many of the interpretations were off base or did not speak to the average person, myself included. A defining moment came when I purchased a short commentary entitled, *The Message of Revelation*, written by Michael Wilcock. The writer, while still over my head, referred to Revelation as a type of drama or play, and by fate or destiny, it was an "ah ha!" moment. I realized that I was finally beginning to understand a book that had scared me to death some thirty-five years earlier. Now when I think about, "What is my purpose? Why am I here?" I can begin to answer the question honestly by saying I am to bring light, understanding, and meaning to the writings of the Holy Scripture, starting right here with a heavenly drama called Revelation.

Two of the greatest gifts God has given me are my stubbornness and ignorance. When reading Revelation, when reading the commentaries, I would not give in to the conclusions many of the authors had arrived regarding the meaning of the book. I did not give up trying to find an interpretation that held deep meaning for those two thousand years ago and also for us today, while at the same time being faithful to the nature of God. In addition, when reading Revelation, when reading the commentaries, I discovered that many of the brilliant minds of the scholarly world speak a language I have difficulty understanding. I found myself reading the research with a dictionary in one hand, scratching my head with the other, wondering what in the heck I had just read. I say it's a gift because now I can put down in writing a faith-filled interpretation of Revelation in a language that I can understand. If I can comprehend, you will understand and hopefully enjoy.

With this stubbornness and ignorance, maybe you don't get the writing style of a Mark Twain or C. S. Lewis. Instead, you receive the best efforts of a simple servant who feels compelled to share with others my journey in discovering the mystery and meaning of Revelation. I promise, if you dedicate the time and effort, four things may occur. First, you will be one of the few who have read the entire book of Revelation. Second, you will learn that many of the so-called "end of time" ranting, whether it be the Nostradamus predictions, the Hopi prophecies, the Bible codes, or even the newfound 2012 predictions have no basis and are simply bull! Third, you will discover this strange book of Revelation is one of the greatest pieces of literature ever written with meaning beyond your imagination and extreme relevance today. Finally, I pray that your life will somehow be changed for the better due to John's vision.

Note to Readers

If we are to do justice interpreting this heavenly drama, we must first determine how we approach the Bible as a whole. There are about as many ways to read the Bible as my golden retriever has fleas. Some claim this sacred book was written by God himself. Others claim it was dictated to individuals through the Holy Spirit and then written down. Some claim it was simply inspired by God herself and put into the hearts and minds of humans. Others claim it was politically motivated. Some claim the book is infallible and without error. There are others who even claim the Bible was simply made up. We debate whether or not Noah's Ark existed, whether or not Jonah could actually live in the belly of a big fish for three days. We try to discover the historical Jesus in order to confirm our belief in the Christ. Like I said, there are many opinions on the bestselling book since the invention of the printing press, but for the most part, they miss the relevance of a one-of-a-kind story.

I may not be the smartest person, but I know the Bible well enough to basically take any subject matter (abortion, death penalty, ordination of women, gay sex, any sex), and argue either *for* or *against* it taking one-liners straight out of the Bible. I am quite certain this is *not* how the Bible is meant to be read. I buy into the philosophy of the sixteenth century reformer Martin Luther—with a twist. Luther once compared the Bible to the manger in which Jesus was born. Think about it! The manger, like the Bible, was built by human hands with the material being supplied by God. However, while God is perfect, we as humans are not! We have flaws in our building projects and confusing statements in our Bible. Yet someway, somehow within the pages of the Bible one finds the Divine, or better put the Divine finds us. Just like in that manger, Luther claimed the Bible holds the Christ, the Living Word, God's address to you! And if the Bible is the living Word of God, it becomes impossible to interpret in a literal fashion, using one liners to prove general truths, because then it would simply be a dead word with one basic meaning only from the past, taking away the true power of God's Word—a divine word inspired by God from the past, but directed as a brand new word to each and every generation, both now and in the future.

After all, when you get right down to the basics, the Bible contains a rather simple message given to us quite clearly in the first book of the Bible called Genesis. I realize I promised the last book of Revelation, but we need the core message of the first book implanted in our hearts and minds if the last book is to make any sense. In Genesis we see God creating all there is and giving you and I this wonderful creation on a silver platter, asking only two things from us: (1) Take care of creation, including one another!(2) See that tree in the middle of the garden? That is the tree of knowledge! Do not eat from it! Trust that I have your best interest at heart! But these two simple commands are too much to ask. We do not take care of creation and each other. We do not trust that God has our best interest at heart. So the rest of the Bible is basically a story calling for you and I to repent and start doing what we have been created to do.

This core belief of Scripture will affect how we approach the study of Revelation. Sure, many of the views I bring to this book are simply that—my views. However, they are insights that brought the Holy Scriptures alive and dramatically changed my life. I do not want you to read the book and simply agree. I challenge you to go deeper because the book of Revelation is one of the most wonderful pieces of literary heavenly artwork ever written. Yet it is more than simply literature, much more. One must realize that truth comes in many different colors, sizes, and shapes, even bizarre symbolism. Revelation will call for not only interpretation but tons and tons of imagination, and here is where today's reader may encounter a slight problem. We simply do not think like people two thousand years ago. We desire to have things spelled out for us, in black and white. We're becoming a society that desires instant gratification with a tendency to avoid things and situations that ask us to go beyond our comfort zone, what we hold as true and holy. We may resist a text or viewpoint that challenges our particular values, so much so that we will not hear the Spirit. So throughout the book, I ask that you place your imagination in gear and "Let anyone who has an ear, listen what the Spirit is saying" (Revelation 2:7, NRSV), because the short writing of Revelation basically uses the entire Bible as reference. In some ways, it is actually a summary of the Holy Scriptures. It pulls many of its ideas from the gospels but hardly contains a verse that in someway does not have some kind of contact with the language and imagery of the Hebrew Scriptures, especially books like Ezekiel, Isaiah, and most of all Daniel.

Throughout the book, I will examine the writings of Revelation, using the New Revised Standard Version (NRSV) and the New International Version (NIV), going not so much chapter by chapter, or verse by verse, but instead by breaking down the story into various sections, which seem to cover different aspects of history. Going verse by verse or chapter by chapter can be helpful to some, but it can also be misleading. One loses the big picture and the imagery the author is trying to display. You see, chapter and verse divisions are not part of the New Testament as it was written. When the New Testament was originally written in Greek, there were no periods or commas. There weren't even spaces between words. Eventually, the Greek was translated into Latin, the language of the

Roman Empire, and remained in Latin until Martin Luther translated the Bible into German in the 1500s. However, in the year 1205, a man by the name of Stephen Langton, a professor from Paris traveling horseback to Lyons France inserted the first chapters and verses into the Latin version of the Bible. His divisions were accepted by a printer in the 1400s and now we have our verses and chapters. So does it make sense we have the separation of verses and chapters where they are located? Yes and no. Yes, because they make referencing and finding passages of Scripture easier. No, because in many cases, the verses and chapters are misleading, tending to take our thought process in the wrong direction. Such is the case with the chapter and verse divisions of Revelation. The proper analysis of any piece of literature, including the Bible, should be according to subject matter. It should arise from a careful and serious study of the text itself. In looking for the natural divisions, I have read the book and listened to it some one hundred times, remembering Revelation is a letter, and it is a vision! "Write in a book what you *see*," the angel will say (Revelation 1:11, NRSV). It is a letter meant to be read and read aloud, and a good reader would make the letter come alive to its hearers, something I believe we need more in our readings on Sunday morning. It is also a vision, a vision in which one can imagine some little house congregation sitting on the edge of their seats, listening and wondering what comes next. If we read and listen to Revelation in this manner, without the chapter and verse, without all the excess interpretation of the past two thousand years, I think we may see certain things in the letter that may surprise us.

On the stage of John's vision, we will notice many actors and actresses coming and going. There is constant movement. However, every so often we come to a point where there seems to be a shift. It's sort of like the curtain falls, a moment goes by and then it rises again. Therefore, I have tried to separate or divide the visions in this manner.

Background of Revelation

Traditionally, the date of the book's writing has been set sometime in the mid-80s or 90s CE. It comes to us some fifty years after the death of Jesus toward the end of the reign of a Roman Emperor named Domitian. The emperor, sort of like the upstanding citizens of North Carolina who persecuted my father, has been recorded in history as taking action against anyone who had different ideas. Stories have it that Domitian would throw huge parties for the leading citizens. Get this! He would run giant stakes up the rib cages of those who would not worship him as a god or bow down to Rome (mostly Jews or Christians). Domitian would then have their bodies wrapped tightly to the stakes, dip them in tar, set them on fire, and use these human torches to provide light for his party guests. Told you we were going to use our imagination. So imagine if the stories are true; one gets a clearer view of the environment the Christians and Jews of those days had to endure.

At the time Revelation was written, as I have mentioned, somewhere between 80 and 90 CE, the Roman Empire was the most powerful government in the world, probably more powerful than the United States of today. As you saw, the empire flexed its muscle in a way that caused many trials and heartaches for the earliest Christians, and the practice of "emperor worship" increased the number of citizens who were forced to make life and death decisions between their religion and government. In this setting Revelation was written to seven towns in Asia Minor and meant to be a circular letter, meaning it was to be read *aloud* in home churches and then passed on to the next community. The message will lay bare the situation, which one will learn is not much different today. The book will point out the causes of our predicament in many and various ways, using symbolic pictures and numeric codes. It will teach what is being done about these problems and will offer a solution to those who are willing to "listen what the spirit is saying." Like I said, it sounds pretty important to me!

So now I ask you to put on your thinking cap full of imagination as we proceed to analyze John's vision. Try to put yourself in John's place and see things the way John sees them because the writer is going to take you places no one has ever been, places so strange and remote many hesitate to go.

What Does Revelation Mean?

The revelation of Jesus Christ, which God gave him to show his servants what must soon take place; he made it known by sending his angel to his servant John, who testified to the word of God and to the testimony of Jesus Christ, even to all that he saw. Blessed is the one who reads aloud the words of the prophecy, and blessed are those who hear and who keep what is written in it; for the time is near.

Revelation 1:1-3 (NRSV)

The first question to address is, what does "Revelation" mean? Revelation is the English equivalence to the Greek word *apocalypse*. We've heard of apocalypse, right? Well, the two are one in the same, and while apocalypse might be to some a scary word, both words simply carry the meaning "to reveal." That's it! If one is talking about religious things, the word begins to take on the meaning of "revealing God's divine secrets and plans for the universe." Revelation is concerned with revealing knowledge not only of the age to come but also revealing important facts about what has happened in the past and what is happening right now. Basically, we are talking about the mysteries of human existence.

The problem or challenge in arriving at a meaningful interpretation of Revelation is that apocalypse in our culture has taken on the meaning in most circles to relate to the end of the world—gloom and doom—the second coming in which all will be destroyed. The church itself has been a huge contributing factor in the misunderstanding of Revelation. It has either avoided the writing for centuries because it doesn't know what to say or doesn't like what the book says. Many churches that happen to teach from this wonderful piece of literature fill us with false doctrine or flat out lies. The futuristic views play on humankind's obsession with the end times. That is why books and movies such as *The Left Behind* series, or the new teaching of 2012 exploit the theme, which fascinates the public. Yet one important fact you must let sink into your mind is the book of Revelation is not simply about the end of times but about the past, the present, and the future.

Despite being the title given to the book, the word *Revelation* is only used in the first line. Nowhere does the word surface again. Everywhere else this piece of literature is known as prophecy, another unique word we tend to misinterpret. Prophecy is greater than just telling the future. Prophecy is the ability to cause the future! In the case of Revelation, the events will come about not because of what John says but because of what God says. The revealed knowledge is not from John. John is simply reporting what he sees. The revealing comes through God, given to Jesus Christ, made known to John only through an angel.

Almost half of the references to angels in the New Testament are found in our writing from John. The Greek word for angel is *angelos,* which simply means messenger, and throughout the Bible, both Hebrew Scriptures and Christian writings, these messengers come in many shapes and sizes. Some may appear as our typical heavenly being we imagine coming to Mary, mother of Jesus. Others may come as a still small voice like to Jeremiah the prophet. The important fact being that there are many ways God communicates with us, just like John. You will most likely be visited by one of these angelic creatures in your lifetime. The question becomes, *Will you notice? Will you listen?* But be very careful because there are even angels or messengers of evil, as we will see later.

Another fact found in the early going is that Revelation is written for all people who claim to be servants or followers of Christ. This is rather unique because the majority of the New Testament is written to a group of people or even to a particular person. Paul writes many of his letters to individuals such as Timothy or Philemon. The author of Luke and Acts addresses his letters or stories to a person called Theophilus. There are books written to the Hebrews, to the people of Rome, and to the people of Corinth. Yet we as modern day readers consider these ancient writings somehow relevant for us today. So how much more should one accept the relevance of Revelation, a book that claims to be written for you?

John—through the angel, through Jesus Christ, through God—is going to *show* you what must soon take place. He's not going to tell you a story as found in the gospels. John is not going to lay out a logical argument as Apostle Paul does in his writings. Like I said, and this is very important—John is going to *show* you what must take place by using a different form of communication called apocalyptic literature. Apocalyptic literature is a type of literature not using logic or story lines to which we are accustomed, but rather tries to persuade, teach, and reveal with words having more than one meaning—symbolic language—once again, forcing us to use our imagination.

So one of the first questions I imagined was, *What must soon take place?* and *What time is near? The end of the world? Isn't that what most people teach us about Revelation? Isn't this the conclusion the so-called "end-time" prophesies try to make you believe?* Yet here the writer does not reveal this knowledge…not yet. After all, what writer in their right mind would give away the plot in the very first paragraph? Yes, I will admit Revelation in some sense deals with what lies in the future, but right now, it says nothing about the end of the world! All we know for certain is this heavenly drama is going to *show* us something only God knows and whatever it is, it is going to happen soon—a lot sooner than we like or imagine.

Last but not least, in the short opening, an angel,

a messenger, states something I've never seen in any writing. "Blessed is the one who reads aloud the words of the prophecy, and blessed are those who hear" (Revelation 1:3, NRSV). This is a promise from God to all who read Revelation aloud. It is a blessed assurance from the Almighty to all who hear Revelation read aloud, and if one believes in the promises found in the Bible, then I think they would be ecstatic to learn not only will you receive an understanding of this bizarre book, but you will be blessed in some way if you read it aloud. Try for a change and trust God—read the text of Revelation aloud!

Who Is the Author?

John,

    To the seven churches in the province of Asia: Grace and peace to you from him who is, and who was, and who is to come, and from the seven spirits before his throne, and from Jesus Christ, who is the faithful witness, the firstborn from the dead, and the ruler of the kings of the earth. To him who loves us and has freed us from our sins by his blood, and has made us to be a kingdom and priests to serve his God and Father—to him be glory and power for ever and ever! Amen. Look, he is coming with the clouds, and every eye will see him, even those who pierced him; and all the peoples of the earth will mourn because of him. So shall it be! Amen. "I am the Alpha and the Omega," says the Lord God, "who is, and who was, and who is to come, the Almighty."

                              Revelation 1:4-8 (NIV)

What an extraordinary beginning! You have a personal greeting from the Holy Trinity—the true author of Revelation. Although the Holy Trinity is not once mentioned in the Scriptures it is a concept developed through passages such as the one just read. Some may think the Trinity is a complicated term, but in actuality, it is a very simple manner of seeing or understanding the ways that God is God. There's God the Father, or Creator, whom we cannot fathom, yet we feel in our hearts the awesomeness, whether one is Christian, Jewish, Muslim, Hindu, or Buddhist. Jesus, on the other hand, separates the other main religions in a special way by giving us a glimpse of this mysterious God. Through the life, death, and resurrection of Jesus we are shown what God is like. The Spirit is the one who calls us, enlightens us, and makes us continue our search for the ultimate meaning and purpose. That is why I boldly claim we have an extraordinary beginning because the reader or listener is personally greeted by God, whom we as Christians call the Father, Jesus Christ, whom we call the Son, and personally greeted from the all-encompassing Spirit that will aid us in understanding Revealed Knowledge—by God.

The Hebrew name for God is Yahweh, or written as YHWH. I appreciate the Jewish tradition, which discourages the speaking of such a Holy Name, and because of our unworthiness, the name of God is only to be spoken by certain people on certain occasions. What I find interesting is the name YHWH, sort of like the book of Revelation, has no tense. YHWH can refer to the past, present, or future, meaning it can be interpreted as "I am who I am," or "I was who I was," or it could mean, "I will be who I will be." So the first greeting comes from God, YHWH the Father *who was, who is, and who is to come*, a beautiful statement which connects all things from beginning to end, and also a statement which will play a vital role later in Revelation. I realize it may be annoying but allow me to repeat, "Who was, who is, and who is to come," will come back and play an important role later in Revelation. We are also sent a personal greeting from the second person of the Holy Trinity, Jesus Christ as prophet, priest, and king. As prophet, Jesus is the faithful witness who *causes* the future with the good news that the Creator cares for you. As priest, Jesus is the first born from the dead who offers himself up as a sacrifice for our sin, giving hope for eternal life. And as king, Christ Jesus is the true ruler of the earth, whether one believes or not. Finally, there is a greeting from the Spirit. Actually, the text claims there are seven spirits, and so right off the bat we have our first encounter with numbers. While the numbers in Revelation may yield some secrets, we must be careful not to go too far. Throughout the book, we will encounter repeated number patterns. The question becomes, *What do they mean and how do they relate to the story?* The number seven occurs throughout the Bible and traditionally it has simply been taken to mean completeness, or all of something. So in the beginning of the text the seven churches of Asia symbolically stand for all the churches in the world, but it must be made clear they also stand for seven real churches. Since the number seven means whole, complete, and full, these seven Spirits are once again the completeness, wholeness of God equally present in all seven churches, or better put, present in every church at all times. I told you this was a spectacular greeting.

Who Is John?

I, John, your brother who share with you in Jesus the persecution and the kingdom and the patient endurance, was on the island called Patmos because of the word of God and the testimony of Jesus. I was in the spirit on the Lord's day, and I heard behind me a loud voice like a trumpet saying, "Write in a book what you see and send it to the seven churches, to Ephesus, to Smyrna, to Pergamum, to Thyatira, to Sardis, to Philadelphia, and to Laodicea." Then I turned to see whose voice it was that spoke to me, and on turning I saw seven golden lampstands, and in the midst of the lampstands I saw one like the Son of Man, clothed with a long robe and with a golden sash across his chest. His head and his hair were white as white wool, white as snow; his eyes were like a flame of fire, his feet were like burnished bronze, refined as in a furnace, and his voice was like the sound of many waters. In his right hand he held seven stars, and from his mouth came a sharp, two-edged sword, and his face was like the sun shining with full force. When I saw him, I fell at his feet as though dead. But he placed his right hand on me, saying, "Do not be afraid; I am the first and the last, and the living one. I was dead, and see, I am alive forever and ever; and I have the keys of Death and of Hades. Now write what you have seen, what is, and what is to take place after this. As for the mystery of the seven stars that you saw in my right hand, and the seven golden lampstands: the seven stars are the angels of the seven churches, and the seven lampstands are the seven churches."

Revelation 1:9-20 (NRSV)

The text tells us Revelation is written by a person named John on the island of Patmos because of the Word of God. Patmos is a desolate volcanic island off the coast of Greece used as a type of Alcatraz, a place prisoners were sent to basically die. A question arising in my tiny mind is, *Is this John the same John who supposedly wrote the fourth Gospel of John? Is this the same John that wrote I, II, and III John of the New Testament?* I don't know, but I do believe there are some strong similarities in the thought process and writing style to at least warrant a serious argument that the writer of the Gospel of John and the writer of Revelation are one in the same person. I realize this would put the apostle around the age of eighty, but stranger things have happened. It's just the more I read, the more I see similarities. But right now we have the reason for the book of Revelation. John is commanded to write down what he sees and send it to the seven churches, which form a large circle in Asia Minor. The purpose, therefore, of Revelation is to inform not only these seven churches, but the universal church what must soon take place!

Over and over again, throughout the Bible, when one is in suffering and imprisonment, when one feels trapped and it looks like things couldn't get any worse—a place we have all found ourselves in at some point in our lives—this is when God comes to us and this is when God comes to John. It is easy to promote a gospel that simply brings blessing upon blessing, but to promote a message of service and sacrifice as John does is a harder gospel to swallow. One's faith in the Son of Man may actually cause one's life to become more difficult. John's suffering and exile for the sake of this hard gospel proves to be the entrance to the gateway of heaven. It is a fact in our lifetime there will be suffering, yet it is through our suffering one sees God.

I mentioned earlier Revelation would test your unused imagination and here is our first clear example. John hears the voice like a trumpet, but what grabs his eye is seven lampstands with something in the middle holding seven stars. We need to rejoice in the fact that we are told the seven lampstands are the seven churches John is to address. I can't stress enough they also represent the universal church, your church, in your hometown. The stars we are told are the seven angels—messengers of the seven churches—and I say rejoice because believe you me, here is about the only time we will be told what a symbol stands for. We are not told flat out who the one standing in the middle might be, but there are times when the meaning in Revelation is quite clear, even though not stated. It is the vision of Christ, and the vision is quite similar to the one found in the book of Daniel of the Hebrew Scriptures. In some cases throughout the story of Revelation, we may be better off not trying to explain every detail. Just think if you tried to explain the details of your dream to another person? The person might think you are nuts. Let's say for right now that John has seen the Christ, a similar vision of the Old Testament, standing in the center of the church with his angels or messengers.

Early on, the vision should begin to adjust our view of reality. On earth, we see the lampstands—the churches—as they appear in the world, congregations located on about every street corner, various denominations with varying messages, which individually can be isolated and destroyed. We have all seen a church or two in our lifetime that has been whisked away for whatever reason. However, in the vision of John, if the Son of Man stands in the center of the church, it will be united and indestructible. If the earthly lampstands proclaim the gospel which has two sharp edges—life and death, salvation and damnation—and Christ remains the focal point in its mission and proclamation, we could eliminate the earthly reality of the church—lamps gleaming here and there across the dark world ever seemingly threatened by conflict and extinction. The church in the heavenly vision could actually become the reality of one, holy, catholic, and apostolic with Christ in the center, giving light to a darkened world we will soon discover.

Who Are the Seven Churches?

Ephesus

To the angel of the church in Ephesus write:
These are the words of him who holds the seven stars in his right hand and walks among the seven golden lampstands: I know your deeds, your hard work and your perseverance. I know that you cannot tolerate wicked men, that you have tested those who claim to be apostles but are not, and have found them false. You have persevered and have endured hardships for my name, and have not grown weary. Yet I hold this against you: You have forsaken your first love. Remember the

height from which you have fallen! Repent and do the things you did at first. If you do not repent, I will come to you and remove your lampstand from its place. But you have this in your favor: You hate the practices of the Nicolaitans, which I also hate. He who has an ear, let him hear what the Spirit says to the churches. To him who overcomes, I will give the right to eat from the tree of life, which is in the paradise of God.

> Revelation 2:1-7 (NIV)

Always remember the blessing to read aloud! As you read through the letters constantly recall, while they are letters addressed to individual churches at a particular time, they are also letters addressed to the universal church in our time—your church today. Your mission, if you choose to accept, is to figure out which letter applies to your congregation and more importantly, what should be done about it.

Ephesus holds a great deal of history. She was a most beautiful city located on the coast of the Adriatic Sea, a city with some 500,000 residents famous for trade, and since she was visited by many travelers, religion played an important role in that culture, not only Christianity but basically every religion known to humankind—from the worship of Aphrodite, Apollo, Hercules, and Zeus, to name just a few.

The book of Acts found in the New Testament teaches the Apostle Paul played a vital part in the early spread of Christianity in Ephesus. So it makes sense in Acts 19:26 the author writes how in Ephesus Paul was brought to trial for ruining the silversmith named

Demetrius' business of supplying idols for all the different religions. Paul stands up among the crowds and states, "gods made with hands are not gods" (NRSV). It is a theme of "idolatry," worshiping things other than God that will resurface throughout Revelation. However, Paul may not have been the only early disciple who had influence in Ephesus. Some historians claim that the Apostle John who may have written Revelation spent years in the city before being exiled to Patmos. Some go as far to pronounce John the first bishop of Ephesus. If that is the case, I'm quite sure the first letter would have gained John's utmost attention.

Even though the early Christians of this city must put up with the different religions of the world, the letter begins with positive feedback. Christ commends them for their zeal because he also hates the false teaching of these so-called Nicolaitans. A group of people also referred to later in the letter to Pergamum, but exactly who are these Nicolaitans? Most scholars seem to agree they are an actual group of people who claimed to have a special type of knowledge. The Nicolaitans would admit that Jesus was a god, after all, there were many gods in that culture, but to this group Jesus was not the Jewish God of the Hebrew Scriptures. This god, the Hebrew God, they taught was evil just like the rest of the world. Weird huh? Salvation or being saved meant escaping from the material world. The odd thing about escaping, it was done by indulging. To them what was done in the body on earth had no bearing on the soul. May sound a little odd to us, yet the ancient teaching is not so much different than the modern belief, "If it feels good, do it!" To make matters worse only those who had this special knowledge could hold the power. A good literal translation of what the word Nicolaitan means would be "those who prevail over the people." I don't mean to be rude, but it seems today many Christians seem to think they too have this special knowledge and use it to manipulate and control—to prevail over the people.

Ephesus, however, doesn't buy into this strange teaching of the Nicolaitans. Her works, toil, and patient endurance are all commended by Christ, especially the value she places on correct teaching. However, it could well be that attitude of sound doctrine leading the church in Ephesus down the wrong path. A serious problem found in many of the churches throughout the world today! In her zeal for the truth, in her desire to make certain right and sound teachings are proclaimed, it seems the church in Ephesus has lost the one thing that is so very important—her love! Christ says, "You have abandoned the love you had at first." All this zeal for truth and concern about keeping the church safe from people who disagree becomes 100 percent meaningless if she abandons her love for God and for one another.

Yet, isn't that the case today? How many lampstands are in the world today like the one in Ephesus? You know a church that is so rigid, so demanding you dare not question or doubt? Sure they may work hard, and it shows, but God forbid if you break any of their so-called rules. Love will go out the door along with you. I've seen churches that will not baptize, marry, give communion, or even bury because they too have this special knowledge, and they use it to manipulate and control—to prevail over the people. For Ephesus, her punishment is harsh! If she does not repent, turn around, and return to the love she once had, the lampstand will be removed. Sadly, it seems she did not take the advice because church and city vanished some one hundred years after the letter of John.

Smyrna

> And to the angel of the church in Smyrna write: These are the words of the first and the last, who was dead and came to life: I know your affliction and your poverty, even though you are rich. I know the slander on the part of those who say that they are Jews and are not, but are a synagogue of Satan. Do not fear what you are about to suffer. Beware, the devil is about to throw some of you into prison so that you may be tested, and for ten days you will have affliction. Be faithful until death, and I will give you the crown of life. Let anyone who has an ear listen to what the Spirit is saying to the churches. Whoever conquers will not be harmed by the second death.
>
> Revelation 2:8-11 (NRSV)

Smyrna is one of the oldest Greek establishments in Asia Minor, dating all the way back to the tenth century BCE, until the Greek population was overrun by the Turkish government in 1923 following World War I. At the time of Christ, when Tiberius was emperor of Rome, he called Smyrna "the most beautiful city of all," which could still be an appropriate statement today. She was known for having a rich and powerful local Jewish community, and it is in this setting John writes knowing they are being persecuted for their beliefs, and they will likely continue in suffering. They did! It was in Smyrna where one of the earliest and most influential church fathers by the name of Polycarp wrote about the tension between the Christian and non-Christian, between the rich and poor. He was executed in 155 CE.

I find it interesting Smyrna is one of two churches that does not receive warning, only praise and encouragement. From the outside looking in, the church would seem to be a struggling congregation. One might think if a certain community followed Christ faithfully, then suffering would be eliminated, right? Once again, isn't that what many churches teach? Isn't that how we attempt to determine the success of churches today? The vibrant and thriving must be doing something right, while the struggling and conflicted churches need to get their act together. Why then should Smyrna, who is being faithful to Christ, undergo such persecution? *What if we have it all wrong?* Does God's control mean that Satan, the evil one, the accuser, the devil is prevented from causing one to suffer? No! In most cases, the opposite is true! When the true work of God is progressing, evil will raise its ugly head even more. Nowhere in the New Testament does it promise freedom from suffering in this life, as many of the so-called churches of prosperity proclaim. Their misleading message is one of the reasons they are full, because all people desire freedom from persecution and suffering, and they will flock to a place that promises a solution, even if it is a false one. However, the one lesson that must be learned from Smyrna is that while suffering for the faith is certain, its time is limited. For her it is only ten days—a short time in the scheme of things—and the suffering will come to an end. Its members will not be harmed by the second death.

Second death? What in the world does it mean by a second death? We don't even know what happens in the first death! Or do we? Well, in the first death, there are only two options. The first option is you die, and that's all she wrote. Your faith or lack of faith didn't matter a hill of beans. I'm not real comfortable with this choice. The second option is that the Bible's claims are true. If its claims are true, and there is a heaven and a hell, then I think it might be wise to invest at least a little time investigating those claims. After all, we have nothing to lose and everything to gain! Yet even through our faith in biblical claims, we can't be exactly certain what happens at the first death. Why? Because even the Bible gives conflicting stories!

Once again there are two trains of thought regarding what happens at the first death, both biblical! First is the teaching that one will not see heaven until the end of time, or until the last trumpet. The Apostle Paul writes in 1 Thessalonians,

> For the Lord himself will come down from heaven, with a loud command, with the voice of the archangel and with the trumpet call of God, and the dead in Christ will rise first. After that, we who are still alive and are left will be caught up together with them in the clouds to meet the Lord in the air. And so we will be with the Lord forever.
>
> 1 Thessalonians 4:16-17 (NIV)

Paul tries to explain this process in another letter written to the people of Corinth by saying,

> Listen, I will tell you a mystery! We will not all die, but we will all be changed, in a moment, in the twinkling of an eye, at the last trumpet. For the trumpet will sound, and the dead will be raised imperishable, and we will be changed.
>
> 1 Corinthians 15:51-52 (NRSV)

Here it's sort of like your first death could be compared to a long nap. If you died tonight and the world ends 10,000 years from now, to you it may seem like a blink of the eye or perhaps a good night's sleep. I'm not extremely comfortable with this option either.

The second option regarding what happens at the first death is the one I hope for and seems to be more biblically sound. We will read in a moment that John sees a great multitude, which no person could count standing before the throne. If one doesn't go to the afterlife immediately, where did this great multitude come from? Once again, the Apostle Paul tries to dance around this question in 2 Corinthians by writing,

> For we know that if the earthly tent we live in is destroyed, we have a building from God, a house not made with hands, eternal in the heavens. For in this tent we groan, longing to be clothed with our heavenly dwelling—if indeed, when we have taken it off we will not be found naked.
>
> 2 Corinthians :1-3 (NRSV)

In essence, Paul is trying to comfort us in the fact that when you die you will not rot in the ground turning pale green until the end of times (naked) but will indeed be clothed with a heavenly body at the point of death. However, my favorite is where Jesus says to the thief on the cross, "Truly I tell you, *today* you will be with me in Paradise" (Luke 23:43, NRSV).

Okay! If the first death is that complicated, what does one do with a second death? It seems throughout Revelation, and is a general consensus in society today, that at some point the world as we know will cease to exist—the end times. According to Christianity, Judaism, and the Islamic faith, when that time comes, there will be a final judgment. It also seems, according to the text, that all those who did not go to paradise following the first death and have been rotting in the ground for the past 100,000 years or more will now have one last chance to plead their case when history ends. Here too is where the idea of purgatory creeps in. However, those who hold fast to the teaching of God, like those in Smyrna, will not be harmed by this "second death," but those of us who do not hold fast and happen to end up before that judgment throne at the end of the world had better hope God is a God of unlimited mercy. Are you frightened just a little? The second death will resurface toward the end of Revelation, and I will cover the topic in more detail, but allow me to ask right now, "Do you really want to take that chance?"

Pergamum

To the angel of the church in Pergamum write:
These are the words of him who has the sharp, double-edged sword. I know where you live—where Satan has his throne. Yet you remain true to my name. You did not renounce your faith in me, even in the days of Antipas, my faithful witness, who was put to death in your city—where Satan lives. Nevertheless, I have a few things against you: You have people there who hold to the teaching of Balaam, who taught Balak to entice the Israelites to sin by eating food sacrificed to idols and by committing sexual immorality. Likewise you also have those who hold to the teaching of the Nicolaitans. Repent therefore! Otherwise, I will soon come to you and will fight against them with the sword of my mouth. He who has an ear, let him hear what the Spirit says to the churches. To him who overcomes, I will give some of the hidden manna. I will also give him a white stone with a new name written on it, known only to him who receives it.

Revelation 2:12-17 (NIV)

Pergamum was a major military outpost and a political center of the Roman Empire. The city had one of the largest libraries in the world catering to the top intellectual Greek minds. She hosted all kinds of famous sporting events, had a famous healing ministry of priests, one named Asclepius who was even considered a god. Here too was an altar built to the god Zeus as the savior, and one of the earliest temples for state-sponsored worship of the emperor, an important fact when one considers the words of Christ referring to the throne of Satan. All this from a Greek culture that stressed the importance of mind and body; in return, all the dominant society of the Roman state asked for was allegiance. Doesn't sound like too much?

In Pergamum, we once again find the presence of the Nicolaitians having that special knowledge, manipulating and controlling the people, teaching what is done on earth has no bearing on the soul—"If it feels good, do it!" The writer references these people back to the Hebrew Scripture and compares them to a character called Balaam. The story of Balaam can be located in the Hebrew Scriptures, a book called Numbers, chapters 22-25. It is about a powerful fortune-teller who attempts to lead the people of Israel into lustful and gluttonous behavior. This misguided adventure is spoiled by one of those messengers (angels) we talked about earlier, and get this—through a talking donkey! However, here in Pergamum the words of Christ sound forth like a "sharp, two-edged sword" not only revealing the truth, one side of the sword, but also punishing evil, the other side of the sword. He promises to use both sides against those who do not repent. But repent from what?

I hope one can begin to understand the situation being addressed not only at Pergamum but in society today. The world offers the church two very difficult choices—give in to what the world has to offer or be persecuted. In the letter to a society such as Pergamum, offering the citizens libraries, sporting events, and many gods, it can be extremely hard on those who refuse to go along, especially when it teaches the "if it feels good, do it" philosophy. Just like in our world today, the distinction between church and society becomes blurred. We have all seen or heard of churches like the one in Pergamum where the city or culture have so much to offer it actually pulls people away from our purpose of worship. You know, soccer games on Sunday morning at nine o'clock a.m., boating after a hard week at the grindstone, family commitments, football at eleven o'clock, and the infamous only day to sleep in. In our society of prestige and wealth, Satan does sit on the throne offering lustful and glutton behavior causing suffering to those who resist, like poor Antipas, a faithful follower whom tradition teaches was slow roasted over the fire inside a brass bull.

Nevertheless, in the end it is always Christ they must deal with because to those who repent, who turn around, Christ will give manna from the Old Testament, or simply what they need on earth. He will also give them a white stone, which in those days could be used as a ticket to enter all the various sporting events of the city, but this particular white ticket from Christ is one to an eternal event.

THYATIRA

> And to the angel of the church in Thyatira write: These are the words of the Son of God, who has eyes like a flame of fire, and whose feet are like burnished bronze: I know your works, your love, faith, service, and patient endurance. I know that your last works are greater than the first. But I have this against you: you tolerate that woman Jezebel, who calls herself a prophet and

is teaching and beguiling my servants to practice fornication and to eat food sacrificed to idols. I gave her time to repent, but she refuses to repent of her fornication. Beware, I am throwing her on a bed, and those who commit adultery with her I am throwing into great distress, unless they repent of her doings; and I will strike her children dead. And all the churches will know that I am the one who searches minds and hearts, and I will give to each of you as your works deserve. But to the rest of you in Thyatira, who do not hold this teaching, who have not learned what some call "the deep things of Satan," to you I say, I do not lay on you any other burden; only hold fast to what you have until I come. To everyone who conquers and continues to do my works to the end, I will give authority over the nations; to rule them with an iron rod, as when clay pots are shattered even as I also received authority from my Father. To the one who conquers I will also give the morning star. Let anyone who has an ear listen to what the Spirit is saying to the churches.

Revelation 2:18-29 (NRSV)

The actual churches receiving the letters would have a pretty good idea of their meaning, because Thyatira had beautiful shrines and temples built to Apollo whose statue actually had eyes of fire. The city also had temples built to the god Helius whose feet were made of bronze. Yet what's disturbing is that Thyatira has a woman named Jezebel. Is this a real woman? I say yes. Is this her real name? Probably not, because in the Old Testament over and over Israel is referred to as the wife of God and any false gods or false prophets are her lovers. On many occasions, we learn that Israel commits adultery with these false gods and prophets—not a sexual act mind you—but being led astray from God, not putting God first! In first Kings 16:31 and 2 Kings 9:22 it is a woman named Jezebel who seduces God's bride (Israel) into a kind of unfaithfulness.

You see, there is a pattern starting to form. The sins of Thyatira are like those at Pergamum. They are both sins of immorality and unfaithfulness connected to idol worship—a theme I mentioned will dominate throughout Revelation. Yet remember idol worship is not simply bowing down to a piece of wood. Idol worship is anything that takes the place or comes before trusting God. Immorality is not simply sexual or behavioral. Immorality is anything that seduces us away from placing God first. How many of us, how many of our churches are guilty of these sins?

There are similarities between Smyrna, Pergamum, and Thyatira. All are being tempted into the trap of idolatry, yet there are important differences as to the manner they are falling into the trap. In Smyrna, if you recall some ill-advised outside religious figures, maybe some right-winged Jews who did the accusing; in Pergamum, Satan the deceiver leads them to immoral behavior or fornication by sitting on the throne. He accuses by using the pressures of the world, society, culture, and state, seducing Christians into worshiping false gods. However in Thyatira, where the church is known for its strength and growth, the damage can be done most effectively, not from outside pressures, in many cases this will only strengthen a strong organization. No, the pressure must come from some type of poison within. Here it happens to be a woman from the congregation who takes on the evil character of Jezebel seducing people away from God by teaching fornication—once again a type of unfaithfulness to God. You must admit, sometimes working from the inside is the best way into the heart of a strong and lively organization. I can't tell you how many times I have seen surges in the growth of a church only to be put down by one or two people doing the work of Jezebel from within. We see it all the time! When some of the TV evangelistic preachers come on the air ranting and raving about a new message, a new way to succeed, blessings to be obtained, they gain immediate success because people can easily be swayed from a gospel calling for sweat and sacrifice to a more attractive Jezebel and her message. However, Thyatira must be very careful because the piercing eyes and trampling feet of Christ will come to her in full strength, much worse than the pagan sun god Apollo, or the Greek god Helius. Yet to those who stay faithful, there are rewards: "To the one who conquers I will give the morning star" (Revelation 2:28, NRSV). Later in Revelation 22:16 it reads, "I, Jesus am the bright morning star" (NRSV).

Sardis

> To the angel of the church in Sardis write: These are the words of him who holds the seven spirits of God and the seven stars. I know your deeds; you have a reputation of being alive, but you are dead. Wake up! Strengthen what remains and is about to die, for I have not found your deeds complete in the sight of my God. Remember,

> therefore, what you have received and heard; obey it, and repent. But if you do not wake up, I will come like a thief, and you will not know at what time I will come to you. Yet you have a few people in Sardis who have not soiled their clothes. They will walk with me, dressed in white, for they are worthy. He who overcomes will, like them, be dressed in white. I will never blot out his name from the book of life, but will acknowledge his name before my Father and his angels. He who has an ear, let him hear what the Spirit says to the churches.
>
> Revelation 3:1-6 (NIV)

Sardis may well be the vaguest letter to the churches. She was a Roman administrative city actually known for its big and beautiful worship places. We know Sardis was a very wealthy community having lavish and huge synagogues complete with gymnasiums and bathhouses. One of the synagogues unearthed through archeological digs had a type of fellowship hall that would accommodate over one thousand people with large marble fountains in the center.

Yet something struck me quite odd about the letter. Up to this point, in spite of all their faults, Christ has recognized the good in the midst of the warnings, but in the letter to Sardis, one needs to ask what does Christ find good here? Not much! Only a few good people and that she had a "good" reputation. In name, she is alive; in fact, she is dead. How true of so many of the churches? All the beautiful marble fountains, large worship spaces regarded by those outside as flourishing, active, successful, all but Christ! Her works do not measure up to what is expected from the church. What was it? We don't know, but I would imagine with all the glitter and glorious buildings, most of her members would be surprised to hear the letter.

I also think many of the churches that seem to flourish in our time would be surprised if they received the same letter. I have attended many of the so-called mega churches with libraries, restaurants, gyms, auditoriums that seat 15,000, offerings in the hundred thousand dollar range per week, and yet something I couldn't put my finger on was missing. Don't get me wrong, I've been in small churches where the same things happen. The point is just because a church seems to be doing well on the outside, many times on the inside she is dead, and for sometimes vague and varying reasons. Have we become more concerned about looks of our buildings and how many people walk through our doors, than the needs of those in our own backyard? Once again, there is that loud call to "turn around!" Can we hear what the Spirit is saying to our church?

PHILADELPHIA

> And to the angel of the church in Philadelphia write: These are the words of the holy one, the true one, who has the key of David, who opens and no one will shut, who shuts and no one opens: I know your works. Look, I have set before you an open door, which no one is able to shut. I know that you have but little power, and yet you have kept my word and have not denied my name. I will make those of the synagogue of Satan who say that they are Jews and are not, but are lying I will

> make them come and bow down before your feet, and they will learn that I have loved you. Because you have kept my word of patient endurance, I will keep you from the hour of trial that is coming on the whole world to test the inhabitants of the earth. I am coming soon; hold fast to what you have, so that no one may seize your crown. If you conquer, I will make you a pillar in the temple of my God; you will never go out of it. I will write on you the name of my God, and the name of the city of my God, the new Jerusalem that comes down from my God out of heaven, and my own new name. Let anyone who has an ear listen to what the Spirit is saying to the churches.
>
> Revelation 3:7-13 (NRSV)

Philadelphia is the second church in which Christ finds no fault. The entire letter is one of encouragement. She is not the rich community of the other cities but more of an agricultural region that was hit hard by one of the world's worst earthquakes in 17 CE. To make matters worse, about the time Revelation was written, history teaches us that the emperor Domitian (remember him—the one using Christians as party lights), in the interest of protecting the vine growers of Italy, required that half of Philadelphia's vineyards planted in the province be cut down and no new ones planted.

There was also a heavy Jewish population in Philadelphia claiming only the Jews were God's children. Yet in the letter Christ reverses the idea that God is for a certain people only, he says, "They will learn that I have loved you" (NRSV). Something we should keep in mind today. This is a bold statement against *any* religion or denomination that claims God as their own. One should begin to notice throughout the book an effort is being made to bring the two faiths together—the established practice of Judaism and the rising beliefs of Christianity—which the writer will claim are one and the same. I also believe through John's writing we should never underestimate the power and love of God to work through *all* faiths. Would our church be surprised to hear Christ say to us in regards to Hindus, Buddhists, and Muslims, "You will learn that I have loved them?"

Even though Philadelphia has seen many trials, the city for years continued to be a place where Christians were fearless in the witness of their faith. For this, Jesus promises those who suffer and are persecuted in this life there is another reversal. Christ will never betray his people like the Roman government. The door has been opened that no one can shut!

Laodicea

> To the angel of the church in Laodicea write: These are the words of the Amen, the faithful and true witness, the ruler of God's creation. I know your deeds, that you are neither cold nor hot. I wish you were either one or the other! So, because you are lukewarm—neither hot nor cold—I am about to spit you out of my mouth. You say, 'I am rich; I have acquired wealth and do not need a thing.' But you do not realize that you are wretched, pitiful, poor, blind and naked. I counsel you to buy from me gold refined in the fire, so you

can become rich; and white clothes to wear, so you can cover your shameful nakedness; and salve to put on your eyes, so you can see. Those whom I love I rebuke and discipline. So be earnest, and repent. Here I am! I stand at the door and knock. If anyone hears my voice and opens the door, I will come in and eat with him, and he with me. To him who overcomes, I will give the right to sit with me on my throne, just as I overcame and sat down with my Father on his throne. He who has an ear, let him hear what the Spirit says to the churches.

Revelation 3:14-22 (NIV)

History and archaeology fill this letter with many interesting facts for the background of the seventh and final church. Laodicea was a banking center, a large textile town known for its wool, producing expensive garments, and famous for the manufacturing of a certain kind of eye ointment. The town was also fed with a type of limewater warm from the ground. Now if one reads back over the letter it should make more sense, and Christ's words to the church would be harshly true. If only you were cold or hot! Ouch! What more terrible situation could there be of a church's condition that the Lord would prefer even a cold Christianity to the kind he finds in Laodicea?

What I find fascinating is the church seems to be a reverse of the city itself. (Yet that shouldn't surprise us because the entire Bible seems to be a reversal of what we hold to be true.) The city is made up of wealthy bankers, physicians, and clothing manufacturers, but the letter claims the church is poor, blind, and naked. The warmness of Laodicea is the worst condition a church can sink. It has all the resources to make a difference in the world, yet seems content to keep the status quo continuing to live as if all is well. How many churches have you seen like Laodicea? A church made up of wealthy members, a budget that can be met by two or three members, a high-paid pastor and so they think like Laodicea all is well. Now that's what I call lukewarm. Their condition is even worse than Sardis where at least a glimmer of life remains, because in the letter one finds some harsh words from Christ. In effect, Jesus says, "You make me sick!" Yet even with the harsh words, Laodicea has a chance. The fact that Christ rebukes her shows he still loves her and even tells her so. The only way to get out of this mess is to let Christ back into the center of her community. So open the daggone door! The good news is that it seems Laodicea did open the door because the next three hundred years the city maintained a strong Christian witness, setting up many of the guidelines the church abides by to this day.

Here ends the letters to the churches. Even though the writing opens with stillness there are a couple of moving topics that surface: The first glaring issue deals with a type of immorality that permeates the churches in various shapes and sizes, causing her to lose sight of her purpose, that of love and forgiveness, with a continuing strong call to repent or turn around. The second topic deals with the ongoing conflict between the Jewish faith and the newly founded Christian faith.

I hope you have noticed while the vision addresses real churches with real problems, the visions are also addressed to all the lampstands throughout the world.

Your task is to figure out what letter is being addressed to you, take the encouragement, advice, and warning as actual letters written to you today. Is your lampstand like the church at Ephesus, Smyrna, Pergamum, Thyatira, Sardis, Philadelphia, or Laodicea? Let anyone who has an ear, listen to what the Spirit is saying to the churches.

Who Are the Twenty-four Elders and the Lamb?

WHAT MUST SOON TAKE PLACE

After this I looked, and there in heaven a door stood open! And the first voice, which I had heard speaking to me like a trumpet, said, "Come up here, and I will show you what must take place after this." At once I was in the spirit, and there in heaven stood a throne, with one seated on the throne!

Revelation 4:1-2 (NRSV)

The curtain comes down! The set is quickly changed, and now I wish I could see what John sees—a door standing open to heaven! He sees the holy throne with someone sitting on it. We assume this someone is God, but not until much later in Revelation 21:1 does the text actually confirm our assumption that the one seated upon the throne is in fact the Almighty. John hears the same voice that contacted him in the first part of the book and now the voice says, "Come up here, and I will show you what must take place after this" (Revelation 4:1, NRSV). Whoa! What in the world does this mean? Of course, it means the future but whose future? Is it John's future, the future of the church, or perhaps your future?

I'm an ex-football player, so I like to think John may have been summoned before the head coach to look at some plays. Try to imagine maybe a big black board in which someone has placed all kinds of Xs and Os. The Xs and Os represent the movement of players and the play's design. Now the movement of the Xs and Os can mean various things. It could mean we are examining the play from the past and seeing what went wrong and what went right. It could be the play that we want to run at this moment, or it could be a play that we want to run in the future, and so we look at all our options. It helps me to think of John's revelation in this manner. These visions can mean either what has already happened, (the past), what's happening now, (the present), or what is about to happen, (the future)—all bound together in a fascinating story! So "what must take place after this" becomes sort of like the playbook, drawing up our options for right now and for the future by examining the past.

Around the Throne

> And the one who sat there had the appearance of jasper and carnelian. A rainbow, resembling an emerald, encircled the throne. Surrounding the throne were twenty-four other thrones, and seated on them were twenty-four elders. They were dressed in white and had crowns of gold on their heads. From the throne came flashes of lightning, rumblings and peals of thunder. Before the throne, seven lamps were blazing. These are the seven spirits of God. Also before the throne there was what looked like a sea of glass, clear as crystal. In the center, around the throne, were four living creatures, and they were covered with eyes, in front and in back. The first living creature was like a lion, the second was like an ox, the third had a face like a man, the fourth was like a flying eagle.
>
> Revelation 4:2-7 (NIV)

In the beginning of Revelation, we saw churches, lamps, stars, and spirits all appearing in groups of seven. Now we see a gorgeous picture combining many of the important images of the Hebrew Scriptures presenting God as the One worthy of praise. Immediately following God's spectacular entrance, we will be introduced to the coming of a new era, Jesus the Christ, once again trying to connect the Jewish tradition to Christianity, but first we see before the throne seven lamps, a crystal sea, four strange living creatures, twenty-four elders, a rainbow, and lighting with thunder. John sees the inner meanings of all these symbols. He sees the majesty, glory, and power of God.

By the time one finishes the book, you should come to the conclusion that the Bible is a wonderful teacher. It is a good teacher because it will repeat its lessons over and over again, in many different ways in order that we may hopefully get the message, and one of the things it seems to repeat are these types of number patterns and bizarre symbols. But what do the symbols and numbers mean?

In the last chapter, we saw the seven lampstands are the church. We know from the Hebrew Scriptures in the story of Noah the rainbow is a sign of God's faithful promise. Lightning and thunder always represent God's presence. The crystal sea is also very interesting. It is from the sea where all chaos and destruction was thought to have come from. I mean it wasn't too long ago humans still thought this way. The earth was flat, and from the sea, one simply fell off the face of the earth. The Old Testament is full of references to the sea being the place of the great chaos monster, but here that chaos is no longer a threat. It has become smooth like crystal glass. Pretty, huh? But what about those numbers? In ordinary life, there are two kinds. There are statistical numbers, which answers the question, "How many?" There are ten people at a meeting. Then there are symbolic numbers that stand for something. For example if your daughter scores a perfect ten at a gymnastics meet, of course it means more than a number. Revelation is like this. The numbers in most cases are meant to mean more than mere counting. Here is no exception. The twenty-four elders are the twelve tribes of Israel combined with the twelve apostles of the Lamb. I say this because the two groups are brought together once again much later in Revelation 21:12-14. The two sets of twelve serve an important purpose in linking the people of God in the Hebrew Scriptures to the people of the same God of the New Testament. The linking is rather important because in early Christianity a huge split arose over the nature of Jesus. Even among the groups agreeing this person was a god, the argument got ugly as to whether Jesus was the same God as the one referenced in the Hebrew Scriptures. The angel shows John that the two are actually one in the same—God of the twelve tribes and God of the twelve apostles. The twenty-four elders represent this coming together of the old and new, Hebrew and Christian, now representing all of God's people. Now picture in your mind all of God's people worshiping at the throne along with four living creatures!

These four strange living creatures have had entire books dedicated to them. Some get so wrapped up in the symbolism the actual meaning fades away. Simply put, the four living creatures stand for everything that is noble, strong, swift, and wise in God's good creation. The lion is king. The ox is strong and serves as sacrifice. The eagle is swift. The human is wise? Yet four living symbols are much more than simply creatures. The Hebrew Scriptures make it perfectly clear that all heaven and all earth show God's handiwork and declare His glory. The four living creatures, therefore, are all of nature, the four corners of the earth—north, south, east, and west. Could not this concept of unity serve us well in today's multicultural, multi-religious world?

Worship

> And the four living creatures, each of them with six wings, are full of eyes all around and inside. Day and night without ceasing they sing, "Holy, holy, holy, the Lord God the Almighty, who was and is and is to come." And whenever the living creatures give glory and honor and thanks to the one who is seated on the throne, who lives forever and ever, the twenty-four elders fall before the one who is seated on the throne and worship the one who lives forever and ever; they cast their crowns before the throne, singing, "You are worthy, our Lord and God, to receive glory and honor and power, for you created all things, and by your will they existed and were created."
>
> Revelation 4:8-11 (NRSV)

This, my friends, is what you call worship! This, is also one very vital reason to attend church or at least find a place to worship, because as we will see, worship is an important part of Revelation. All living creatures, all of nature, and later all heavenly creatures worship the One on the Throne. All will bow down sooner or later! Here we see worship and praise because of gratefulness, because of God's worthiness. Later we will witness worship through fear and trembling.

One should notice also that singing hymns to God, worshiping God and the Lamb, is totally opposite from idolatry, a theme we saw in the letters to the churches. Worship, one will learn, involves a specific type of behavior, and those who worship eventually take on a particular lifestyle. One cannot have true worship of God and still worship the beasts, who will be introduced later. Worship is an expression of worthiness, glory, and honor. It should not become an escape from life and from our witness. If so, it has lost touch with its purpose. Of course, our religious activity can be a type of safe haven from the rigors and temptation of everyday life. It can also be a social gathering of like minds and a means of resisting our dominant culture, but when worship serves merely as a drug or a high for our personal use, a painkiller for the hurt of life, rather than a divine discipline for serving and praising the only One who deserves this worship, we have moved into an area that is contrary to God's purpose. Worship must be done from the heart, out of the same sense of the twenty-four elders and the four living creatures. Our purpose in life is to be like the twenty-four elders and four living creatures who day and night without ceasing they sing. They sing of the glory of God and live out that glory by placing their gold crowns at the feet of God.

THE SCROLL

> Then I saw in the right hand of the one seated on the throne a scroll written on the inside and on the back, sealed with seven seals; and I saw a mighty angel proclaiming with a loud voice, "Who is worthy to open the scroll and break its seals?" And no one in heaven or on earth or under the earth was able to open the scroll or to look into it. And I began to weep bitterly because no one was found worthy to open the scroll or

to look into it. Then one of the elders said to me, "Do not weep. See, the Lion of the tribe of Judah, the Root of David, has conquered, so that he can open the scroll and its seven seals." Then I saw between the throne and the four living creatures and among the elders a Lamb standing as if it had been slaughtered, having seven horns and seven eyes, which are the seven spirits of God sent out into all the earth. He went and took the scroll from the right hand of the one who was seated on the throne. When he had taken the scroll, the four living creatures and the twenty-four elders fell before the Lamb, each holding a harp and golden bowls full of incense, which are the prayers of the saints.

Revelation 5:1-8 (NRSV)

Now John sees the One sitting on the throne with a scroll sealed with seven seals. What is the scroll with seven seals? Well, the text will answer the question later. Let me just say something extremely important. Revelation chapter five is a pivotal part in the book. Listen up! Of all creation, who is worthy to open these seals and show us the events that must take place? Of all of creation, who is worthy to open these seals and explain our past, present, and future, our history and our purpose? Of all creation, there is no one...but one!

With what has happened so far, one might want to picture some powerful, mighty, awesome, bigger-than-life type character to be the only one in the history of the world to explain what is called life but *no*! What John sees is a Lamb! A Lamb that looks like it has already been slaughtered! So contrary to what we might have been thinking, a weak creature with no mark of power—only the mark of death—is the only One worthy to be the agent of God's purposes. The Lamb stands between the One sitting on the throne (God) and the four living creatures (nature) serving as a type of bridge between heaven and earth. The Lamb is the one who clearly shows the true nature of God, yet in the same breath, the Lamb still deserves the exact same praise as the one on the throne. Beautiful, huh?

As I mentioned earlier, chapter five brings together the story of the Hebrew Scriptures into the teachings of the New Testament. To center stage comes Jesus to take and open the sealed scroll. On the heavenly stage, John sees the lionlike greatness, the absolute power of God with his seven horns, symbols of strength and the wisdom of God with his seven eyes watching over all creation. Yet to us, here on the earthly stage all we see is something that looks like a slaughtered Lamb.

John is allowed to see thousands and thousands of angels or messengers join in the worship with the twenty-four elders and the four living creatures. All things, earthly and heavenly will praise the One on the throne and also the One like a Lamb.

The Song

> They sing a new song: "You are worthy to take the scroll and to open its seals, for you were slaughtered and by your blood you ransomed for God saints from every tribe and language and people and nation; you have made them to be a kingdom and priests serving our God, and they will reign on earth." Then I looked, and I heard the voice of many angels

surrounding the throne and the living creatures and the elders; they numbered myriads of myriads and thousands of thousands, singing with full voice, "Worthy is the Lamb that was slaughtered to receive power and wealth and wisdom and might and honor and glory and blessing!" Then I heard every creature in heaven and on earth and under the earth and in the sea, and all that is in them, singing, "To the one seated on the throne and to the Lamb be blessing and honor and glory and might forever and ever!" And the four living creatures said, "Amen!" And the elders fell down and worshiped.

Revelation 5:9-14 (NRSV)

Like I said, that's what one calls worship!

What Are the Seven Seals?

SEAL ONE

> I watched as the Lamb opened the first of the seven seals. Then I heard one of the four living creatures say in a voice like thunder, "Come!" I looked, and there before me was a white horse! Its rider held a bow, and he was given a crown, and he rode out as a conqueror bent on conquest.
>
> Revelation 6:1-2 (NIV)

The worship and praise of the Lamb brings about a voice like thunder from nature, or the four living creatures announcing the "four riders of the apocalypse." Who are these riders? Many believe they know the answer to this riddle. I have been informed over and over the four riders bring the end of the world. So-called scholars, books, and movies have claimed and written that the four riders of the apocalypse are the bearers of gloom and doom, and when they arrive, existence as we know it will cease. Yet remember, the entire book is about revealed knowledge (past, present, future), and here is no different, because as you will see shortly, they are simply four riders that have been riding out since the beginning of time, they are riding now and they will ride in the future.

So let's begin with the first rider. We might be very confused about the identity of the rider on the white horse if it were not for Revelation 19:11-16, where a crowned conqueror, again, appears riding a white horse. Here, late in the book, the rider is identified as Faithful and True, as King of Kings and Lord of Lords. His name is called the Word of God. Therefore, I say with confidence the rider of the first white horse is none other than Christ, the embodiment of God's eternal message—the gospel!

Two things happen when I make this statement. If in Revelation as I claim the four horsemen have been riding out since the beginning of time, now and in the future, we have an important feature of the first rider, the Lamb, Jesus the Christ, the gospel. It means that Christ did not come into existence as many think—two thousand years ago—but has been around since the beginning of creation. It also means when human beings came into existence the gospel was born—the gospel or "good news" that we are to take care of this wonderful creation—plants, animals, earth, sky, each other, and trust that the One seated upon the throne has our best interest at heart. As the writer of John's Gospel states in 1:1 and 1:14, "In the beginning was the Word...and the Word became flesh and lived among us" (NRSV). In essence, Jesus was, is, and is to come; he holds the same job description as the Almighty—with a touch of skin. Also since one can say with confidence that the first rider is the Christ—Word become flesh—the gospel, then one can begin to establish that the symbolism in Revelation will hold true and steady throughout its message. Seven will always be complete. White horse, white stone, white robes will always relate to Christ and his eternal gospel. The bizarre symbolism will start to take on consistent meaning, enabling us to begin our interpretation with understanding.

The first rider represents Christ with the spread of the conquering gospel and the conquering gospel has two sides. Just like the sharp, double-edged sword coming from the mouth of Christ in the letter to Pergamum—truth offering life or death. On one side we are conquered; on the other side, we conquer. For those who accept its message, the rider has a crown—life—but for those who reject the conquering message there awaits a bow—death. The most important question asked thus far, and will be repeated throughout the book is, *How does one respond to the first rider of Christ and the eternal Word of God?*

SEAL TWO

> When he opened the second seal, I heard the second living creature call out, "Come!" And

> out came another horse, bright red; its rider was permitted to take peace from the earth, so that people would slaughter one another; and he was given a great sword.
>
> Revelation 6:3-4 (NRSV)

The second horse is bright red like the bloodshed caused by war. Its rider has a great sword, not two-sided mind you but only the side of death. It is a vision not only of war, but of murder and terrorism, conflict, and strife. The second horseman riding out is a type of division between humans caused when the gospel is accepted by some and rejected by others. The conflict began all the way back in the beginning of human existence when Cain killed his own flesh brother Abel, over the worship of the One sitting on the throne. The bright red bloodshed has never ceased! Once again, the conflict is caused by our response to the first horseman, the Word of God. Basically, every war and conflict in human history has in some way involved the acceptance or rejection of the gospel. Remembering the good news, the gospel and the Lamb have been around longer than Cain or Abel.

SEAL THREE

> When the Lamb opened the third seal, I heard the third living creature say, "Come!" I looked, and there before me was a black horse! Its rider was holding a pair of scales in his hand. Then I heard what sounded like a voice among the four living creatures, saying, "A quart of wheat for a

> day's wages, and three quarts of barley for a day's wages, and do not damage the oil and the wine!"
>
> Revelation 6:5-6 (NIV)

The third rider represents an economic situation. At first, it sounds like it could refer to famine or widespread scarcity because the verses talk about a ration of corn for a full day's wages, or more of a lesser quality of food at the same price. Sort of like the street person with a sign claiming, "Will work for food." Times are hard! However, notice the supply of olive oil and wine is not affected. One should say these commodities represent the luxuries, the caviar and champagne, perhaps even three square meals a day, which in the hardest times still furnish the tables of the rich and famous, still furnish our tables. We live in a world today where nearly one billion people struggle to physically survive because of malnutrition, and as many as *30,000 children die per day* of hunger related causes. Yet most of us capable of reading this book live in a totally different world of olive oil and wine. The third rider on the black horse stands for a time of great economic inequality. The black darkness of injustice ride out and the scales are thrown out of whack. Why?

SEAL FOUR

> When he opened the fourth seal, I heard the voice of the fourth living creature call out, "Come!" I looked and there was a pale green horse! Its rider's name was Death, and Hades followed with him; they were given authority over a fourth of the

> earth, to kill with sword, famine, and pestilence, and by the wild animals of the earth.
>
> Revelation 6:7-8 (NRSV)

Hopefully we can begin to see the results of turning away from the eternal gospel—war, terrorism, famine, and economic injustice, all of which lead to death. And now the fourth rider has the power to wipe out a quarter of the human race. Yet where in the text does it say the slaughter is a single catastrophe? Nowhere! From the beginning of time or recorded history, up to 25 percent of all human beings die from the results of these riders—war, murder, poverty, and disease. These are the deaths and casualties caused by the unnecessary evils of the world constantly riding out as we ignore and resist the first rider—the Word of God! Like I said, the four horsemen are not a prediction of the future as some have us to believe. They are not a representation of the end of the world but a clear vision of what has happened in the past, what is happening now, and what will happen in the future if we continue along the same path.

So in light of the One sitting upon the throne commanding us to take care of creation, in light of the Lamb commanding us to love one another, we should begin to see the overall meaning in the heavenly drama of Revelation. What does the future hold? It holds the same things the past has held, the same things our present holds. It holds the conquest of God's Word constantly riding out on the white horse proclaiming a message of love, forgiveness, justice, and mercy. It holds strife, conflict, murder, and war riding out on bright red horse. It holds economic injustice and scarcity riding out on the black horse. Finally, it holds death on the pale green horse. However, listen up. These horsemen are not the end. All this is but the beginning of what Jesus the Lamb calls birth pains.

Too often we use these signs of terrorism and war, of famine and plague, to predict the end times, but Jesus tells us no! The events of the first four seals we all must live through and like I said, while some believe those to be signs of Christ's return and the close of the age, they are in fact unfortunate commonplaces in history. The four riders of the apocalypse have been riding over the earth from that day to this day and will continue to do so. It is Christ Jesus, the unlikely candidate, that has unsealed the book of history, and what one sees is a world that is suffering, just like that poor Lamb before the throne.

Some believe and teach at least those followers of the Lamb should be exempt from all the suffering of the world. I call it the gospel of prosperity. Yet one will learn very quickly in the fifth seal our suffering, even as Christians, is inescapable. So what's the point one might ask?

Seal Five

> When he opened the fifth seal, I saw under the altar the souls of those who had been slaughtered for the word of God and for the testimony they had given; they cried out with a loud voice, "Sovereign Lord, holy and true, how long will it be before you judge and avenge our blood on the inhabitants of the earth?" They were each given a white robe and

told to rest a little longer, until the number would be complete both of their fellow servants and of their brothers and sisters, who were soon to be killed as they themselves had been killed.

Revelation 6:9-11 (NRSV)

One must keep in mind the conditions that the early Christians were called to exercise their faith. They were asked to choose between Caesar and Christ. If they chose the Lamb, there was a good possibility they would wind up as lion food or party lights. So now we are introduced to the martyrs who have given their lives and would represent all who suffer in any way for/ or on account of God and the Lamb. The inhabitants of the earth or those who dwell upon the earth as referenced in other versions of the Bible , is one of those catchphrases holding deep meaning, and will resurface on many occasions. It does not simply mean humanity in general but refers to those who are completely content with the status quo. It refers to those who simply 'inhabit the earth', taking up space making no useful contribution to the Word and witness of God. These are the ones who do nothing to fight against the red or black horses riding out. These are the inhabitants of the earth who do not battle against strife and injustice. They simply dwell!

Remember earlier when we talked about John seeing heaven, the place where God resides? In heaven, the truth is known. John can now see everything in black and white, truth, lies, good, and evil. In heaven, one can see those who are at home in the present world order or those who are very comfortable with the way things are going. No need for drastic changes. In heaven, one can also see those who hold to Word and witness of God. Therefore, one is either a citizen of heaven or simply an inhabitant of the earth. Which are you?

Those who hold to Word and Witness are given white robes and asked to rest a little longer. Rest a little longer for what? Remember these are the souls who have suffered for the sake of Christ and they are already in heaven. These are the souls under the altar who have seen the first four horsemen riding out, and guess what? They still have say-so as to the outcome of history. It sounds like we may have a voice in heaven when all is said and done. The souls under the altar cry out for judgment in this evil world now seeing things from a heavenly perspective. I don't believe their cry is a cry for personal vengeance but a prayer for justice, and we will learn their prayers are heard.

SEAL SIX

> When he opened the sixth seal, I looked, and there came a great earthquake; the sun became black as sackcloth, the full moon became like blood, and the stars of the sky fell to the earth as the fig tree drops its winter fruit when shaken by a gale. The sky vanished like a scroll rolling itself up, and every mountain and island was removed from its place. Then the kings of the earth and the magnates and the generals and the rich and the powerful, and everyone, slave and free, hid in the caves and among the rocks of the mountains, calling to the mountains and rocks, "Fall on us and hide us from the face of the one seated on the

> throne and from the wrath of the Lamb; for the great day of their wrath has come, and who is able to stand?" After this I saw four angels standing at the four corners of the earth, holding back the four winds of the earth so that no wind could blow on earth or sea or against any tree. I saw another angel ascending from the rising of the sun, having the seal of the living God, and he called with a loud voice to the four angels who had been given power to damage earth and sea, saying, "Do not damage the earth or the sea or the trees, until we have marked the servants of our God with a seal on their foreheads."
>
> Revelation 6:12-7:3 (NRSV)

Now we're going to put our brains into gear. It seems like the prayers of those under the altar are being answered and we come to a crucial point in history. "The great day of their wrath" in the sixth seal ushers in the end of the world as we know it. Let me repeat, the great day of wrath comes in the sixth seal, very early in the book of Revelation. Bear with me. Toward the end of Jesus' ministry on earth the disciples in Matthew 24:3 ask Jesus, "Tell us, when will this be, and what will be the sign of your coming and the end of the age?" Jesus goes on to answer them how they will hear of wars and how there will be famines and earthquakes. This Jesus claims is "but the beginning of the birth pangs." (Matthew 24:8, NRSV) However, he concludes the discussion of the end times by saying in Matthew 24:29, "The sun will be darkened, and the moon will not give its light; the stars will fall from heaven, and the powers of heaven will be shaken" (NRSV). Sound familiar? There is a string of biblical references not only in Matthew, but also Mark and Luke describing very similar details of these last days. The question of whether the earthquake, the darkened sun, and the falling stars should be taken literally to predict an actual time of oblivion misses the point. If on the other hand, one regards these horrific times as simply symbolic, they too miss the point. The important lesson to learn here is that day, the great day of wrath will spell the end of the entire world as we know it, and it will come soon—a lot sooner than we expect or desire.

When I first began to realize what the vision was trying to teach, I was a little confused, wondering why the end was so early in the vision. Should not the end of the world come at the end of the book? But as I will mention over and over again, the Bible is a wonderful teacher because it will repeat its lessons over and over again in many different ways in order that we may hopefully get the message. Here is no different. We will encounter the end throughout many portions of the book. Let's just say for right now in this section the world has been given the message of God—to take care of creation, yet because of us turning away from this gospel and not trusting that the Creator has our best interest at heart, we encounter war and injustice. Even the followers of the Lamb will suffer as the saints before suffered, now crying out for justice. And justice will be served! The end will come! In Revelation, it comes right here and now!

However, before the day of wrath something extremely important takes place. We turn our attention to the ones who are sealed. We turn our minds to those servants of God marked with a seal on their foreheads. Who are they, and why is the sealing important? We are sealed with the promises of God and marked on the forehead as Christians or followers of the Lamb when we are baptized. From those moments forward our ultimate safety is assured when we *use* this gift. When the horsemen of the apocalypse ride out, when the winds begin to blow the servants of God are found to have been sealed against their power, not against suffering, but against their ultimate power. In looking back, we can say that while the horsemen ride out in a destructive path the church and the ones inside, those who have been sealed have been made indestructible—because of our baptism and because Christ stands in the midst of the churches.

> And I heard the number of those who were sealed, one hundred forty-four thousand, sealed out of every tribe of the people of Israel: From the tribe of Judah twelve thousand sealed, from the tribe of Reuben twelve thousand, from the tribe of Gad twelve thousand, from the tribe of Asher twelve thousand, from the tribe of Naphtali twelve thousand, from the tribe of Manasseh twelve thousand, from the tribe of Simeon twelve thousand, from the tribe of Levi twelve thousand, from the tribe of Issachar twelve thousand, from the tribe of Zebulun twelve thousand, from the tribe of Joseph twelve thousand, from the tribe of Benjamin twelve thousand sealed. After this I looked, and there was a great multitude that no one could count, from every nation, from all tribes and peoples and languages, standing before the throne and before the Lamb, robed in white, with palm

> branches in their hands. They cried out in a loud voice, saying, "Salvation belongs to our God who is seated on the throne, and to the Lamb!" And all the angels stood around the throne and around the elders and the four living creatures, and they fell on their faces before the throne and worshiped God, singing, "Amen! Blessing and glory and wisdom and thanksgiving and honor and power and might be to our God forever and ever! Amen." Then one of the elders addressed me, saying, "Who are these, robed in white, and where have they come from?" I said to him, "Sir, you are the one that knows." Then he said to me, "These are they who have come out of the great ordeal; they have washed their robes and made them white in the blood of the Lamb. For this reason they are before the throne of God, and worship him day and night within his temple, and the one who is seated on the throne will shelter them. They will hunger no more, and thirst no more; the sun will not strike them, nor any scorching heat; for the Lamb at the center of the throne will be their shepherd, and he will guide them to springs of the water of life, and God will wipe away every tear from their eyes."
>
> Revelation 7:4-17 (NRVS)

There are a lot of questions and debate regarding those protected or sealed, especially since John hears the number of 144,000. Some have gone as far to claim heaven is limited to the first 144,000. If that is the case, I'm totally screwed! Probably you too! Hopefully, these fanatics are wrong! Remember if one takes literal the Word of God, it loses meaning. A question that helps clear up the issue is not focusing upon who are the

144,000, but who is the great multitude? Because to this question, we are given the answer! It is God's servants! Therefore, we have no reason to limit the ones sealed, either through baptism or through the Jewish faith. Here, surrounding the throne of the Almighty, we clearly find the servants of God, all of them, the Hebrew faith represented by the twelve tribes of Israel and the Christian faith represented by the great multitude. The plain fact of the text says if we are God's servants, we have been sealed.

We spoke earlier about symbolism in numbers. Here is one of those fascinating cases. Put yourself in John's shoes. What he *hears* is a voice from heaven declaring a number, 144,000. The total is a symbolic number but a good one.

There is a beautiful story found in the first book of Genesis 32:24-32. It deals with a person named Jacob, who swindles his twin brother and then deceives his father into giving him the family inheritance. While on the run, Jacob finds himself in a wrestling match with God. During the night struggle, Jacob holds his own until God pops out his hip socket. God then turns to Jacob and says, "You shall no longer be called Jacob, but Israel, for you have striven with God" (Genesis 32:28, NRSV) This scoundrel ends up becoming the father of the twelve tribes included in the 144,000 we just heard. However, since the name Israel simply means "one who wrestles with or strives for God," we now, because of the Lamb, not only include the faithful from the twelve tribes of Israel, but multiply and dramatically increase heaven with the faithful coming from the testimony of the twelve apostles, who also strive for God. Therefore, those John sees worshiping before the throne would include (the twelve tribes of Israel) times (the twelve apostles) equals 144. Toward the end of Revelation, we will learn about the 1,000-year reign of Christ or the existence of the church, which is constantly adding more and more to the great multitude and making the symbolic number of 144,000 gather even more meaning. Told you it was a good number! John *hears* 144,000! Yet he *sees* a great multitude that no one can count! From God's standpoint, they are all Israel! Remember Revelation is a symbolic narrative using various number combinations and pictures pointing back to the same thing, trying its hardest to combine the two faiths. The number and the picture therefore include any and all people from the beginning of time to the end of time who trust and strive for God's purposes in taking care of this wonderful creation. The ones sealed come from every nation under heaven.

Another question we need to ask from this passage is, "What qualifies the ones who have been sealed to stand before God's throne?" The text tells us they have washed their robes in the blood of the Lamb and emerge from suffering. You and I have been given the world on a silver platter to enjoy and take care of, but we fail! We have been asked to trust, but instead we go after God's knowledge. What's needed is a new starting point, and we receive that new starting point through forgiveness! The entire story of the Bible—Hebrew and Christian—is exactly the new beginning we need. Over and over in the Bible, one learns of people just like you and me who try and fail. Over and over, one learns of God's mercy and forgiveness. Yet the people do not accept this gift of forgiveness as a manner to get back on track, so the Lamb of God becomes the promise of forgiveness and mercy in the flesh. From the cross the slaughtered Lamb cries out, "Father, forgive them; for they do not know what they are doing" (Luke 23:34, NRSV). When one accepts the forgiveness offered from the One seated upon the throne, their robe is now washed clean in the blood of the Lamb! When their robe is washed clean, a person's life begins to change taking on meaning and purpose. Now through the blood of the Lamb, shed from the cross, you are the one who is numbered among that great multitude! You have been cleansed from your old life of sin (a past event), been given a new life of witness which no trial can extinguish (a present event). These are the ones God will guide to springs of living water and wipe away every tear from their eyes (a future event).

Revelation is a book about the past, the present, and the future! Revelation does not promise that Christians are insulated against trouble! Seals one through four testify to that, along with the dead martyrs of seal five. Yes, we will suffer, the church will suffer, and there will be no escape from this suffering until the world ends in seal six. However, whether that time comes tomorrow or a million years from now, we, as ones who have been sealed, will not be harmed. Our eternal safety is never in question! The Christian has hope that no one can take away, an inner security trusting they have One sitting on the throne who will protect and forgive. This hope and trust cannot be affected by anything—even the beasts that will rise up before us, even the end of the world. We will stand before the throne, and there will be no more hunger, no more thirst.

SEAL SEVEN

> When the Lamb opened the seventh seal, there was silence in heaven for about half an hour.
>
> Revelation 8:1 (NRSV)

Don't you just love it? The more I read this strange and wonderful book, the more I am convinced that no earthly being could come close to writing this heavenly piece of literature. We have gotten a quick peek at the end times, and they are not pretty. However, it's really not the end of time. There is something more! There is a seventh seal revealing something special. But right now there is silence. Concerning what happens after the end of the world, the Lamb has nothing to say. Right now, we along with John can catch our breath for about a half hour.

How Does God Warn?

And I saw the seven angels who stand before God, and seven trumpets were given to them. Another angel with a golden censer came and stood at the altar; he was given a great quantity of incense to offer with the prayers of all the saints on the golden altar that is before the throne. And the smoke of the incense, with the prayers of the saints, rose before God from the hand of the angel. Then the angel took the censer and filled it with fire from the altar and threw it on the earth; and there were peals of thunder, rumblings, flashes of lightning, and an earthquake. Now the seven angels who had the seven trumpets made ready to blow them.

Revelation 8:2-6 (NRSV)

As each act ends, having traced history to the end and beyond, a new vision returns to a similar beginning, not only reinforcing what we have already learned, but also revealing something new about God's plan. Though some people tend to view Revelation as a type of historical book which outlines detailed accounts covering events that simply occur between the first coming and the second coming. Yet the Bible is not a history book and any historical interpretation will result in misinformation and contradictions. Then there are some who view Revelation as a fortune-telling book predicting a literal fulfillment of its prophecies. This method of straight-line literal interpretation limits the power of Scripture and misses the heavenly drama of the story. The tendency of both types is to read the entire book and assume that the order runs from beginning to end. Revelation does not read like this! It is more like a well thought out novel or play with flashbacks filling in the missing pieces, slowly developing an all-encompassing story. The message of Revelation is meant to reveal the nature of the world by showing visions depicting various stages of heavenly history. The seals taught what will happen throughout history. The trumpets now proclaim a warning to an unbelieving world. The trumpet visions begin precisely at the same point the seal visions left off. While the seals teach us what must happen in the world, the trumpets teach us the ways through which God attempts to warn and save the world.

If you remember back to when Christ opened the fifth seal, John saw under the altar the souls of those who had been slaughtered because of the word of God. They cry out with a loud voice, "Sovereign Lord, holy and true, how long will it be before you judge and avenge our blood" (Revelation 6:10, NRSV). Now we see the altar with the prayers of these saints rising up like the smoke of incense. The prayers are for justice and in this scene we will join John's vision with thunder, lightning, earthquakes—all signs of God's presence—and learn that God hears their prayers and hopefully we will begin to understand how God answers those prayers.

Throughout history, people have taken the signs of their times and inserted them with the trumpet texts. What I find fascinating is that human nature has consistently viewed natural disasters in relationship to the gods, and maybe in some weird way this view is not totally flawed. Think about it. When no one knew God in the Hebrew Scriptures, the Almighty sent the great flood at the time of Noah. Is that a good thing or a bad thing? I mean does one truly desire to live in a world when all people are continually evil? Does God at times use nature to cleanse? Or do these acts of natural disaster enable us to realize that it is not we who control our destiny? Either way one must admit what one finds in the trumpet act is beyond our complete understanding or control. What it does accomplish is the fact that we must pay close attention to the signs of nature in interpreting how we are doing in our relationship to the Creator and creation itself.

One last thing I would like you to ponder while reading this section. The warnings are real and harsh! They may even make us wonder about the nature of God. Yes, I will admit that God's wrath is not something to take lightly, but listen up! God's wrath is not always caused directly by God, but many times by us! By turning away from the eternal gospel and the presence of the One seated on the throne, we ourselves bring on the warnings of the trumpets.

Four Trumpets

> The first angel blew his trumpet, and there came hail and fire, mixed with blood, and they were hurled to the earth; and a third of the earth was burned up, and a third of the trees were burned up, and all green grass was burned up. The second angel blew his trumpet, and something like a great mountain, burning with fire, was thrown into the sea. A third of the sea became blood, a third of the living creatures in the sea died, and a third of the ships were destroyed. The third angel blew his trumpet, and a great star fell from heaven, blazing like a torch, and it fell on a third of the rivers and on the springs of water. The name of the star is Wormwood. A third of the waters became wormwood, and many died from the water, because it was made bitter. The fourth angel blew his trumpet, and a third of the sun was struck, and a third of the moon, and a third of the stars, so that a third of their light was darkened; a third of the day was kept from shining, and likewise the night.
>
> Revelation 8:7-12 (NRSV)

I combined the four angels (messengers) together with their trumpets because I feel certain events at the time Revelation was written would have tempted the reader at that time to do the same. Following the death of Christ and the birth of Christianity, it was pretty much accepted that the second coming was soon, and I mean soon like next week, next year. Some Christian communities would sell or give away all they owned, forsake husbands or wives, and why not, if the end is near. The people of the first century had clear signs from nature that would have reinforced their fears or hopes the end times were near. In 62 CE and again in 64 CE earthquakes rocked the world of the early Christians. A historian by the name of Pliny wrote about the earth cracking open and how the springs and wells dried up. Then right around the time Revelation was written, in the same area, Mt. Vesuvius erupted in the year 79 CE. While the writer Pliny died, his student, Pliny the Younger, reported spewing ash, smoke, and flames rose up into the sky like a giant mushroom cloud blocking out the sun during the day, the moon and stars at night. Fire and debris rained from the sky for eighteen hours. So much so that buildings began to collapse and people frantically ran to the hills and caves seeking cover. The aftermath of this eruption resulted in large brush and forest fires, ships burning in the harbors where the water became unfit for drinking and the ash covered the skies for weeks. Now read back over the four trumpets and imagine. Yes, time is near! Like I said, there have always been times in history where one could be tempted to insert the trumpet texts as warning the end of the world may be coming to an end. For example in 1201, the deadliest earthquake in history killed approximately one million people in Egypt and Syria—I'm certain they believed the end of time was near. Twenty million people died of the black plague. Do you think there may have been some concern? How about WWI or WWII? Many thought it was time to say good-bye. Even recently with the tsunami in Indonesia—watching that wall of water approaching would have convinced me that time was real near. However, one must remember the words of Jesus in Matthew 24:4 where he says, "Beware that no one leads you astray..." (NRSV). Jesus goes on for sometime describing similar events in Revelation, but he finishes by saying, "About that day and hour no one knows, neither the angels of heaven, nor the Son, but only the Father" (Matthew 24:36, NRSV). One should be careful of any theory about the future, which attempts to predict the end-times. The only thing we can do is examine the signs and realize time is getting near.

Revelation is a heavenly story about the past, present, and future, but this does not mean the interpretation will not change from the past to the future or from various points of history. Sure there will normally be grave concern for any period living through natural disasters, and maybe, just maybe we are to use these natural signs to teach that we live in a fragile world where the trumpets may blow at any time. Maybe too, these occurrences in history need to teach us that we are not in control of our eternal fate and therefore, start paying more attention to the first rider on the white horse. However, if one attempts to interpret the text in today's time, I believe we may learn some valuable lessons.

First notice the damage of the first four trumpets affects—the earth, the oceans, the rivers, and the air. Therefore, the important aspect in the first trumpet is that the hail, fire, and blood symbolize any kind of destruction at any time that damages the earth on which we live. Notice it is a partial destruction of our earthly resources leading to many other consequences, such as food shortages, lumber shortages, and grazing shortages, affecting numerous areas of our earthly environment.

In the second warning, the fouling of the seas and destruction of marine life is another aspect of this environmental damage like the damage to the earth in the first trumpet, yet here the warning moves to seas, not only damaging again our ability to produce food but also affecting aspects of trade and commerce.

The third trumpet, I find rather interesting. In the Hebrew Scriptures, the Lord exclaims to the prophet Amos,

> But you have turned justice into poison and the fruit of righteousness into wormwood.
>
> Amos 7:12b (NRSV)

In Jeremiah, the Lord says,

> Because they have forsaken my law that I set before them, and have not obeyed my voice or walked in accordance with it, but have stubbornly followed their own hearts and have gone after the false gods, as their ancestors taught them. Therefore, thus say the Lord of hosts, the God of Israel: I am feeding this people with wormwood, and giving them poisonous water to drink.
>
> Jeremiah 9:13-15 (NRSV)

Hear or see any similarities? In the third trumpet, all

the fresh waters, the rivers, the lakes, basically all our drinking waters will be affected. It even talks about them being bitter, once again a truth containing more than one interpretation. Sure it represents the real water as a natural resource, necessary for earth life which has been turned to wormwood due to pollution—lack of justice. Yet symbolically the living water of the gospel is sweet and holds everlasting life because the Word of God means life and justice. But for those who reject the gospel, its words taste bitter, like wormwood and many die.

The fourth trumpet affects the sun, moon, stars, day, and night. In essence, our atmosphere is being ruined! The ash and smoke from Vesuvius that blocked out the sun and the stars causing little difference between day and night is once again approaching with an even deadlier reality of pollution and global warming. Why is it that smog hovers over our cities like a killing cloud and one can no longer see the stars at night?

Some may think the trumpets blowing do not sound like a gracious God, but remember the damage is partial (one third) not total, which shows us that the trumpets are not yet sounding doom, but serious warning. One could even say in a strange sort of way and should say the miseries of the trumpet are really acts of kindness from God! The first four trumpets give signs that things are going amuck. They show the wicked world being offered mercy and chance for repentance or change. We see fearful damage being done to the earth with strip mining and cutting down of our trees, affecting our vegetation. Our oceans of commerce are being used as garbage and oil dumps, killing its inhabitants. The lakes catch fire and water must now be purified in order to drink. The air we breathe is causing cancer, and our atmosphere is being destroyed. We live in a time where global warming and the threat of nuclear holocaust remind us we may not be eternal. Yet we must understand these are merciful warnings from the One who sits upon the throne. The sad part according to the text, the offer of mercy is not accepted and the world will not repent. However, let it never be said that God has not done all in His power to bring humans to their senses, even to allowing devastation of His own once good earth.

The Fifth Trumpet

> Then I looked, and I heard an eagle crying with a loud voice as it flew in midheaven, "Woe, woe, woe to the inhabitants of the earth, at the blasts of the other trumpets that the three angels are about to blow!"
>
> And the fifth angel blew his trumpet, and I saw a star that had fallen from heaven to earth, and he was given the key to the shaft of the bottomless pit; he opened the shaft of the bottomless pit, and from the shaft rose smoke like the smoke of a great furnace, and the sun and the air were darkened with the smoke from the shaft. Then from the smoke came locusts on the earth, and they were given authority like the authority of scorpions of the earth. They were told not to damage the grass of the earth or any green growth or any tree, but only those people who do not have the seal of God on their foreheads. They were allowed to torture them for five months, but not to

kill them, and their torture was like the torture of a scorpion when it stings someone. And in those days people will seek death but will not find it; they will long to die, but death will flee from them. In appearance the locusts were like horses equipped for battle. On their heads were what looked like crowns of gold; their faces were like human faces, their hair like women's hair, and their teeth like lions' teeth; they had scales like iron breastplates, and the noise of their wings was like the noise of many chariots with horses rushing into battle. They have tails like scorpions, with stingers, and in their tails is their power to harm people for five months. They have as king over them the angel of the bottomless pit; his name in Hebrew is Abaddon, and in Greek he is called Apollyon. The first woe has passed. There are still two woes to come.

Revelation 8:13-9:12 (NRSV)

I find it fascinating the Bible does not distinguish between eagles and vultures. So instead of a majestic creature flying overhead, think of maybe like a vulture circling over a dying world, crying, "Woe, woe, woe to the inhabitants of the earth." The only hope of this passage is that the woes are directed to those who "dwell on the earth." Remember it does not refer to all humanity, but those who take the present world for granted and who feel the earth is theirs for the taking, as opposed to those who hold to the Word and witness of God and believe the earth is the Lord's. The sin which will bring doom is the refusal to heed the warnings given to all people, and our refusal to respond to the first horseman, which is flesh become Word—the gospel.

So let's start with the star falling from heaven. The earth opens up and smoke like a great furnace rises. The keeper of this bottomless pit is an angel (messenger), and his name in Hebrew is Abaddon, in Greek, he is called Apollyon. There is a lot of baggage wrapped up in these two little words. Abaddon means "became lost, ruined, destroyed, perish." It is a poetic word used to symbolize the place of the dead with a most dominant meaning of, "place of destruction." Abaddon is a place of mystery hidden from human eyes but clearly known by God in Job 26:6 and Proverbs 15:11. It has come to be a place of punishment reserved for the wicked. So one could very easily call Abaddon, hell! Here, this hell has been personified and made into something with a name—a name like Abaddon or Apollyon.

Apollyon carries the same meaning in Greek as Abaddon does in Hebrew, only with a kicker. The Greek god Apollo is the god of death and pestilence, and the verb means to destroy. Also Domitian who was most likely the emperor at the time Revelation was written, the one who liked to throw parties using Christians as light fixtures, he also liked to be regarded as Apollo incarnate. What a play with words, huh? So death and pestilence will rise up from a mysterious place only known by God punishing the wicked and bringing destruction.

Okay! Let's interpret the passage literally. Imagine a star crashing into the earth and a great hole opening up somewhere with smoke pouring from it. Sound good so far? Now from the smoke comes a plague of locusts, such as never before seen, armed like scorpions, shaped like horses, crowned like kings with the faces of men, the hair of women, the teeth of lions, armor-plated, winged and moving with a deafening noise. They attack people instead of vegetation, and they are smart, able to distinguish between Christians and non-Christians.

You see, Scripture forbids us interpreting the passage in a literal manner. The important thing about the locusts is not how such creatures could exist, but what do they mean? Sure there are literal locust-plagues found in the Old Testament (Exodus 10:12-20 and Joel 1) and even these demonic creatures have spiritual significance. Simply put, if you think the locusts of destruction and death are bad in the Old Testament wait till you see these buggers. Their appearance is something we have a difficult time imagining, but their effect will be plain sheer terror for quite some time.

Revelation is trying to link the horrible locusts with the many-shaped ills coming in all kinds of packages that will torment the unbelievers in the last days, which even death will not relieve. These locusts will sting with chronic hardships, multiple diseases such as the world could never imagine. Our destruction of land, oceans, rivers, and air will cause the demonlike locusts to rise up from the earth, ready to sting. The many ills are the locusts of trumpet five led by the angel or messenger of destruction, and believe you me, it will not be pretty. Such is the warning of trumpet five and the first of the woes directed against unbelieving people.

Should this passage bother you? Look through it

again. The introduction to the fifth angel informs us that the remaining woes will affect only those who "dwell on the earth." The torturing times will affect those who do not have the seal of God upon their foreheads. Which begs me to consider once again the eternal importance of having one's robe washed in the blood of the Lamb! However, does that mean one simply *claims* to be a Christian? Remember in the beginning of this strange book, we saw that worship was a very important aspect of heaven, and the worshipers eventually take on a particular lifestyle; one cannot worship the One on the throne and still be committing adultery and idolatry. If your robe is washed in the blood of the Lamb, you may very well suffer on earth, but you will not be made to endure the torture of trumpet five. Is your robe washed in the blood of the Lamb? If not, you may someday be a witness to these strange devil-like locusts.

The Sixth Trumpet

> Then the sixth angel blew his trumpet, and I heard a voice from the four horns of the golden altar before God, saying to the sixth angel who had the trumpet, "Release the four angels who are bound at the great river Euphrates." So the four angels were released, who had been held ready for the hour, the day, the month, and the year, to kill a third of humankind. The number of the troops of cavalry was two hundred million; I heard their number. And this was how I saw the horses in my vision: the riders wore breastplates the color of fire and of sapphire and of sulfur; the heads of the

> horses were like lions' heads, and fire and smoke and sulfur came out of their mouths. By these three plagues a third of humankind was killed, by the fire and smoke and sulfur coming out of their mouths. For the power of the horses is in their mouths and in their tails; their tails are like serpents, having heads; and with them they inflict harm. The rest of humankind, who were not killed by these plagues, did not repent of the works of their hands or give up worshiping demons and idols of gold and silver and bronze and stone and wood, which cannot see or hear or walk. And they did not repent of their murders or their sorceries or their fornication or their thefts.
>
> Revelation 9:13-21 (NRSV)

A great deal of truth can be found in the blowing of this particular horn. Trumpet six is the last warning for the inhabitants of the earth. When trumpet seven sounds, it will be too late! Once again, do we take the armies to be literal? Snake-tailed horses with lions' head breathing smoke and fire coming out of the Middle East? Could it now be Iran? Could it once have been Russia, or maybe in the future China with their two billion people? The death-dealing horsemen of trumpet six could be tanks, planes, and bombs but not only tanks, planes, and bombs. They may be these, but more. They are wars and terrorism. They are murders, cancers, and road accidents killing one-third of humankind, more than the seals. Yet even here, the ones that survive must not see any connection, because they still do not repent of idolatry or worshiping things other than God. We hear of pollution ruining our air, of a booming economy that still allows millions of children to starve, of resources that are being depleted, and of blind politicians and leaders who care more about fame and fortune than the well-being of God's good creation and a love we must never abandon. Yet in the end we are promised by the sixth trumpet, those who do not have the seal of God upon their foreheads will be affected by this destruction caused by their worship of demons, or false gods. Their lives will become a torment! The locusts have been let out in trumpet five, but nothing seems to change the minds of those who do not believe. Now in trumpet six, the cavalry rides out to slay with destruction and still the people of the earth hear nothing.

It is from the altar the church's prayers go up and God's fiery answer is sent down. In trumpet six we see, or at least imagine that God is sounding the warning against sin, now run amuck in reply to the prayers of saints that evil should not and will not go unpunished and justice should and will be done. God's last and most potent warning is to be one of destruction and death from these fiery warriors.

Have you noticed throughout Revelation the loud noises—the shouts, the thunder—all trying to get our attention? God whispers to us in our pleasures, speaks to us through our consciences, but God shouts to us in our pain and suffering. If we will not hear the tremendous voice of God sounded through the angels or messengers, sounded through the four living creatures, being shouted out in so many ways there will be no hope for us, what else is God to do? Make us mindless zombies with no freedom to obey or disobey? Then we would not be human! Therefore, God shouts to us through our pain and suffering with signs from nature, visions from prophets, and even through His only Son—the eternal gospel.

The Sixth Trumpet

And I saw another mighty angel coming down from heaven, wrapped in a cloud, with a rainbow over his head; his face was like the sun, and his legs like pillars of fire. He held a little scroll open in his hand. Setting his right foot on the sea and his left foot on the land, he gave a great shout, like a lion roaring. And when he shouted, the seven thunders sounded. And when the seven thunders had sounded, I was about to write, but I heard a voice from heaven saying, "Seal up what the seven thunders have said, and do not write it down." Then the angel whom I saw standing on the sea and the land raised his right hand to heaven and swore by him who lives forever and ever, who created heaven and what is in it, the earth and what is in it, and the sea and what is in it: "There will be no more delay, but in the days when the seventh angel is to blow his trumpet, the mystery of God will be fulfilled, as he announced to his servants the prophets." Then the voice that I had heard from heaven spoke to me again, saying, "Go, take the scroll that is open in the hand of the angel who is standing on the sea and on the land." So I went to the angel and told him to give me the little scroll; and he said to me, "Take it, and eat; it will be bitter to your stomach, but sweet as honey in your mouth." So I took the little scroll from the hand of the angel and ate it; it was sweet as honey in my mouth, but

> when I had eaten it, my stomach was made bitter. Then they said to me, "You must prophesy again about many peoples and nations and languages and kings."
>
> Revelation 10:1-11 (NRSV)

The angel we see resembles the Word become flesh of chapter one. He recalls the promises of the rainbow and points us back to that eternal gospel, the little scroll. There is no need to write it down. It has already been written. It should have been clear to us from the beginning who created the heaven, the earth, and the sea. It should have been clear to us from the beginning our responsibility in the overall scheme of things. There have been warnings given over and over again, but now there will be no more delay. Time has come to an end! The next event in God's calendar will be trumpet seven, and folks that's all she wrote! The mystery of God is found in the little scroll of the gospel, the great radical news of how any person may be reconciled to God through Christ. Yes, there is no need to write this down!

Like I said, the scroll is the gospel. I think we can admit its words at first do taste sweet as honey. The promise of eternal life, inner peace, and the power of the Holy Spirit to guide our lives? How sweet does that sound? Like honey, huh? But once we have digested these words and realize what our response should be, that of standing up in a crowd to condemn injustice, possible separation from our friends and family, a life of trying to love those who hate us, not worshiping the things we think give us happiness! Once we realized what we are called to do as "citizens of heaven," instead of "inhabitants of the earth," the gospel message is bitter and makes us sick to our stomach. Even still, guess what? We are not only called to live out the message of the little scroll, but we are called to prophesy and speak to others about the truth of the scroll, helping to actually cause the future! Ouch, uh? Has your robe been washed?

THE SIXTH TRUMPET

> Then I was given a measuring rod like a staff, and I was told: "Come and measure the temple of God and the altar and those who worship there, but do not measure the court outside the temple; leave that out, for it is given over to the nations and they will trample over the holy city for forty-two months."
>
> Revelation 11:1-2 (NRSV)

While most of this section is about the world, once again there is a little reminder about the safety and security of the church. Insofar as this vision is concerned, the temple means the church, while the city stands for the world. We find those who are sealed and serving God in the temple. Those in the outer court of the temple, perhaps those who claim to worship the Lamb but their actions prove otherwise, are not to be included. They will be given over to the world. Yet the ones who do the works of God are safe. The passage should remind us of the reality that there is a limit to God's patience. Six trumpet blasts represent every possible chance for repentance God offers to humankind, but even with this said, it is not so much the patience of God that we are concerned with but humankind's ability to respond. Finally, humankind has hardened beyond the possibility of repenting, or changing, sort of like in the time of Noah. This will be the day when the angel swears that trumpet seven will no longer be delayed.

The Sixth Trumpet

"And I will grant my two witnesses authority to prophesy for one thousand two hundred sixty days, wearing sackcloth." These are the two olive trees and the two lampstands that stand before the Lord of the earth. And if anyone wants to harm them, fire pours from their mouth and consumes their foes; anyone who wants to harm them must be killed in this manner. They have authority to shut the sky, so that no rain may fall during the days of their prophesying, and they have authority over the waters to turn them into blood, and to strike the earth with every kind of plague, as often as they desire. When they have finished their testimony, the beast that comes up from the bottomless pit will make war on them and conquer them and kill them, and their dead bodies will lie in the street of the great city that is prophetically called Sodom and Egypt, where also their Lord was crucified. For three and a half days members of the peoples and tribes and languages and nations will gaze at their dead bodies and refuse to let them be placed in a tomb; and the inhabitants of the earth will gloat over them and celebrate and exchange presents, because these two prophets had been a torment to the inhabitants of the earth. But after the three and a half days, the breath of life

> from God entered them, and they stood on their feet, and those who saw them were terrified. Then they heard a loud voice from heaven saying to them, "Come up here!" And they went up to heaven in a cloud while their enemies watched them. At that moment there was a great earthquake, and a tenth of the city fell; seven thousand people were killed in the earthquake, and the rest were terrified and gave glory to the God of heaven. The second woe has passed. The third woe is coming very soon.
>
> Revelation 11:3-14 (NRSV)

Midway through this section, we run into a difficult part of the book where John writes about two witnesses prophesying for 1,260 days. Some interpreters, wrongly, I might add, have once again promoted a literal fulfillment of this section. They claim at some time in the future, most likely in Jerusalem, there will be a three-and-a-half-year preaching career of two remarkable people. After these two remarkable people complete their preaching career in the future, they will die a horrible death, and then all will witness their resurrection, resulting in the rapture and end times. Yet Revelation is not a fortune-telling novel. It is a truth story about our past, present, and our future. The two witnesses declaring God's truth to the "inhabitants of the earth" are very simply the witnesses of the Jewish faith and newly founded Christian faith! Here is another picture or symbol for us to play with. Please remember, the vision is constantly trying to unify the message of the Hebrew Scriptures and the teachings of Jesus into one simple Revelation from the One who sits on the throne. We know this because part of the vision shows us the work of God through the prophets found in the Old Testament, with Elijah pouring out fire and shutting off the rain from the sky and Moses with authority to turn water to blood. Then we see or hear the testimony of the New Testament through the witness Jesus the Christ. The two witnesses it says will testify for 1260 days, and if you're any good at math, you will notice is the same amount of time as the forty-two months in which the nations will trample the earth. The two are one in the same, teaching the church will testify and the world will resist. We are starting to see Revelation consistently using different symbols to point toward the same thing! Here we are taught the battle will continue for forty-two months, 1260 days, which not by chance equals the three-and-a-half years of Jesus' earthly ministry, all relating to the time the gospel will be proclaimed, to the time the lampstands will promote the message of the Lamb, to the time the two witnesses will prophesy—pointing back to the three-and-a-half years of Jesus' earthly ministry, a ministry proclaiming unity and love of God for all people. But in the same breath, the 1260 days, the forty-two months, the three-and-a-half years will also be the time in which the gospel will be resisted. So whenever we hear the gospel being preached in the world through words and action, we know that we are still living in the midst of the two witnesses. However, and this is a big however, when the gospel ceases being proclaimed, when the two witnesses are dead or when the church *seems* to perish, we will have arrived at the end times, or the three-and-a-half days of suffering which the text tells us can be seen in the same or worse light as Sodom where no one knew God and Egypt when she was at her worst. At the time when the gospel is no longer being proclaimed, we will see the end of history, and the church to all eyes will seem to go under. Yet the text once again tells us it will be as brief as the suffering of Christ, only three-and-a-half days from his arrest, crucifixion, burial, and resurrection.

Get this! I love this part. While the inhabitants of the earth laugh and celebrate, the church will rise again to meet the Lord, and the world in confusion will at last give worship to its Creator. It is not the willing worship of love we saw in scene one, but the grudging worship of compulsion and defeat, of fear and trembling. The seals showed how the church will suffer, yet be indestructible. The trumpets show how the world will be warned, yet unrepentant. Are you starting to get the feeling there might be something to this strange book after all?

The Seventh Trumpet

> Then the seventh angel blew his trumpet, and there were loud voices in heaven, saying, "The kingdom of the world has become the kingdom of our Lord and of his Messiah, and he will reign forever and ever." Then the twenty-four elders who sit on their thrones before God fell on their faces and worshiped God, singing, "We give you thanks, Lord God Almighty, who are and who were, for you have taken your great power and begun to reign. The nations raged, but your wrath has come, and the time for judging the dead, for

rewarding your servants, the prophets and saints and all who fear your name, both small and great, and for destroying those who destroy the earth."

Revelation 11:15-18 (NRSV)

If no one has heard the loud voices being shouted since the beginning of time, they will hear them now! The second coming has arrived again, just like back in seal six. While the first coming of Christ has affected some, the second coming will affect all. This is the final and overwhelming display of the majesty of God. The entire scene has been a warning to an unbelieving world and if the world has still not repented after the first six trumpets, then trumpet seven will bring the end, whether you believe or not. It is the final woe because from it there is no appeal. Trumpets one through four proved God's power over the earth, which we are so graciously allowed to inhabit. Yet many do not fear or respect God's creation and obey His commands. We have seen over and over again the painstaking lengths the One seated upon the throne will go through to warn. If they hear not the first six trumpets, neither will they repent when trumpet seven is blown. All this is brought about by an answer to the prayers of the saints that wickedness should not go unpunished, and it will not! We pray for justice to be done, and justice will be done. Our dislike for this section of the book is really little more than blindness to the situation. We are destroying God's creation and resisting the testimony of the first rider.

Who Are the Characters of Good and Evil?

Then God's temple in heaven was opened, and the ark of his covenant was seen within his temple; and there were flashes of lightning, rumblings, peals of thunder, an earthquake, and heavy hail.

    A great portent appeared in heaven: a woman clothed with the sun, with the moon under her feet, and on her head a crown of twelve stars. She was pregnant and was crying out in birth pangs, in the agony of giving birth. Then another portent appeared in heaven: a great red dragon, with seven heads and ten horns, and seven diadems on his heads. His tail swept down a third of the stars of heaven and threw them to the earth. Then the dragon stood before the woman who was about to bear a child, so that he might devour her child as soon as it was born. And she gave birth to a son, a

> male child, who is to rule all the nations with a rod of iron. But her child was snatched away and taken to God and to his throne; and the woman fled into the wilderness, where she has a place prepared by God, so that there she can be nourished for one thousand two hundred sixty days.
>
> Revelation 11:19-12:6 (NRSV)

Wow! Isn't that one beautiful piece of literature? What does it mean? Believe it or not, if one invests a little time and lots of imagination, I feel we can find meaning relevant for not only John's time, two thousand years ago, but we can find meaning that is truly relevant for all time. We will learn that, through the birth and ascension of Christ Jesus, all existence has been affected, even heaven! Any question of God's ultimate authority has been tossed out of heaven. The war has been won! However, the battles will continue to be fought on the earthly level.

We along with John are back in heaven and in the presence of God. Heaven is not some place of perfection, but a place where right and wrong, where good and evil can be seen clearly. Through the presence of God with all the forces of nature, the lightning, thunder, earthquakes, hail, and as always, loud noises trying to get our attention, we see the ark of God's covenant, or the promises of God, and will learn what must soon take place. First the scene needs to be set and the main characters introduced.

So who are these strange characters entering John's vision? It says the woman and the dragon are portents—portents being symbolic figures with meaning beyond the ones we see on the surface. They do not represent a literal woman or a literal dragon. The text itself tells us that. They represent something much more. The third character, the child is not a portent or symbol because the child actually represents a human.

The text tells us the dragon is the ancient serpent who is called the devil, which means the one who slanders, and also Satan, which means the adversary, the accuser. The old serpent is the one who deceived Adam and Eve into not trusting God. The old serpent is the oldest form of evil, personified as cunning and wicked, and has enormous power to deceive. *The dragon is evil!* His seven crowned heads show us how much authority evil truly has over us. Ten horns, which are even more than the Lamb, make us believe that the dragon has more strength than Christ himself.

I mentioned earlier the entire text of Revelation is riddled with reference to the Hebrew Scriptures. Here is another example, which is important for us to grasp the feel of the dragon. In Psalm 74:13, there is a dragon with several heads, and this dragon is given a name, Leviathan. More important, Leviathan is used as a symbol of Israel's ancient enemy Egypt. Also the trumpet-plagues in the last section closely resemble the plagues of the Exodus where the Israelites were enslaved by Egypt. Here we see how the woman flees to the wilderness, once again, like the Israelites in the Exodus. We saw in the last section the city, which oppresses God's people is called Egypt. So one could say the dragon is a symbol of Egypt from the Exodus, but more.

The city, which oppressed God's people, is also

called Sodom, where not a single righteous person was found as in the days of Abraham and Lot. So one could say the dragon is a symbol of Sodom, but more.

Later we will hear the angel call out, "Fallen, fallen is Babylon the great" (Revelation 18:2, NRSV) in reference to the beast. Babylon is the city who destroyed Jerusalem and took its inhabitants into captivity around 587 BCE. So one could say the dragon is a symbol of Babylon, but more.

At the time John is writing, Rome has just burned Jerusalem to the ground, and it is Rome now feeding members of the church to the lions, hanging them on stakes, and burning them as party lights. So one could say that Rome is the dragon, but more.

The dragon is much more than simply cities or nations that oppress God's children. The dragon is a powerful system of evil that tends to show its ugly face the clearest in powerful empires and the message it teaches of whatever time, but more.

The serpent or dragon is one who has accused, slandered, and has been our adversary since the beginning of our existence. It is this force of evil that seems to have seven heads and ten horns. It is the one who keeps tempting us into not trusting God and taking care of creation—including each other. This system of evil grows and gains power the more we resist the first rider with the everlasting gospel. I believe we misunderstand and severely limit the force of evil when we simply call it Satan, the devil. Evil or the dragon is very real and very powerful gaining strength as time goes on. We'll discuss more about the dragon later in this chapter.

The woman could logically be seen as Mary, the mother of Jesus, but she is not simply Mary. The woman is also Israel with her exodus to the desert. Her flight into the wilderness is odd enough a place of safety and protection until the end of her 1,260 days, which means the existence of the church. The woman is also adorned with the splendor of sun, moon, and twelve stars parallel to the Old Testament, once again representing the whole family of Israel. What's more is that the woman continues to exist even after the child is gone. So the woman now becomes the "people of God," or the Christian church. She is in fact the old Israel (144,000), the Christian church (the multitude), and also the human woman Mary. And the church will be protected for 1260 days, forty-two months, 3-1/2 years, or as long as the gospel is being proclaimed.

The child is not a portent or a symbol as I mention. The child is the Christ child destined to rule all nations. What I find rather odd is here we have the greatest event in the history of the world summarized in one simple sentence showing us the birth of Christ at Bethlehem, and then the ascension. "And she gave birth to a son, a male child, who is to rule all the nations with a rod of iron, but her child was snatched away and taken to God and to his throne" (Revelation 12:5, NRSV). That's all! Why not more? Because the life, death, and resurrection are what make up the gospel lessons or the little scroll, and if you remember, my friends, there is no need to write it down because it has already been written. Nothing more needs to be said! The important facts in the summary are the birth and the ascension into heaven, because it is between these two points, very important moments in history where God puts Himself within the dragon's grasp and conquers evil forever.

The War in Heaven

And war broke out in heaven; Michael and his angels fought against the dragon. The dragon and his angels fought back, but they were defeated, and there was no longer any place for them in heaven. The great dragon was thrown down, that ancient serpent, who is called the Devil and Satan, the deceiver of the whole world he was thrown down to the earth, and his angels were thrown down with him. Then I heard a loud voice in heaven, proclaiming, "Now have come the salvation and the power and the kingdom of our God and the authority of his Messiah, for the accuser of our comrades has been thrown down, who accuses them day and night before our God. But they have conquered him by the blood of the Lamb and by the word of their testimony, for they did not cling to life even in the face of death. Rejoice then, you heavens and those who dwell in them! But woe to the earth and the sea, for the devil has come down to you with great wrath, because he knows that his time is short!" So when the dragon saw that he had been thrown down to the earth, he pursued the woman who had given birth to the male child. But the woman was given the two wings of the great eagle, so that she could fly from the serpent into the wilderness, to her place where she is nourished for a time, and times, and half a time. Then from his mouth the serpent poured water like a river after the woman, to

> sweep her away with the flood. But the earth came to the help of the woman; it opened its mouth and swallowed the river that the dragon had poured from his mouth. Then the dragon was angry with the woman, and went off to make war on the rest of her children, those who keep the commandments of God and hold the testimony of Jesus. Then the dragon took his stand on the sand of the seashore.
>
> Revelation 12:7-18 (NRSV)

Okay? So when did this war in heaven arise and when did evil get thrown down to the earth, or better yet when was evil conquered in heaven? First, we need to remind ourselves of the characters. The child is the Christ. The woman is originally Israel, God's people, and now the Christian church. The dragon is personified as evil, the ancient serpent, Satan, or the devil. Now appearing for the first time is Michael the archangel who according to Daniel 10:21 is the heavenly champion of Israel or the woman. The conflict is between Michael and his angels and the dragon and his angels. The war, therefore, is between the messengers of evil and the messengers of good. The war is the old and ancient conflict between God and the devil. But something happens at the birth of this one child, the Christ. While in the grasp of the dragon, from his incarnation to ascension, this one human being does what no other human being has ever done. Jesus has loved and trusted God with his entire heart, soul, and mind. He has loved his neighbor as himself. He has kept the teachings of God in a manner no one has been able to keep and because of this Jesus has defeated evil. Even the most feared evil of all cannot overcome what Jesus the Lamb has accomplished. Jesus the Christ defeated death! The most monstrous evil of all time has been tossed out of heaven at the end of the three-and-a-half days where Christ suffered, died, and rose for you! The war is being fought during the time Jesus is in the grave, and it is at his resurrection and ascension that the dragon, evil, or any question of God's ultimate reign is tossed out of heaven. Death has finally been conquered for us to see, and heaven is now secure. God truly is showing us what must soon take place!

However, earth remains a place for the dragon's work! Yet one thing is for certain, the Lamb has suffered all there is to suffer, and he has risen from the grave. The dragon has definitely been tossed out of heaven. Realizing the predicament, the forces of evil pursue the woman, who is now the church. The dragon will do anything possible to sweep her away, but God promises to protect the woman just like God protected the Israelites in Egypt causing the waters to dry up so the people cross safely.

Are you beginning to realize Revelation is a heavenly story portraying great truth, where all readers can find validity for their own experience, no matter what day and age they live? Listen up! For those who love God there can be nothing which God does not provide a way out, a new Exodus, not even death! The dragon has been thrown out of heaven! Alleluia! Yet remember, the dragon is ticked off, and who does he or she take it out on? The ones who trust God and love others, the ones who take care of creation, the ones who witness to others about the slaughtered Lamb—these are the ones who will bear the wrath of the dragon.

People often ask me, "Why does it seem like bad things happen to good people and the wicked in the world seem to thrive?" Lots and lots of books have been written on this subject, but it boils down to the work of the demonic system of evil. Remember when I mentioned that in heaven one of the characteristics was good could be seen for good, and evil could be seen for evil? I don't believe it is so much that the system of evil picks out individuals and makes them suffer, but the dragon stands on the shore just waiting to make use of the sea, which if you recall is the symbol of chaos. Evil will jump all over the opportunity when it sees chaos and confusion enter our lives, patiently waiting its turn to tempt each one of us just as the serpent tempted Adam and Eve.

Where Do The Forces of Good and Evil Collide?

THE BEASTLY INSTITUTION

And I saw a beast coming out of the sea. He had ten horns and seven heads, with ten crowns on his horns, and on each head a blasphemous name. The beast I saw resembled a leopard, but had feet like those of a bear and a mouth like that of a lion. The dragon gave the beast his power and his throne and great authority. One of the heads of the beast seemed to have had a fatal wound, but the fatal wound had been healed. The whole world was astonished and followed the beast. Men worshiped the dragon because he had given authority to the beast, and they also worshiped the beast and asked, "Who is like the beast? Who can make war against him?" The beast was given a mouth to utter proud words and blasphemies and to exercise his authority for forty-two months. He opened his mouth to blaspheme God, and to slander his name and his dwelling place and those who live in heaven. He was given power to make war against the saints and to conquer them. And he was given authority over every tribe, people, language and nation. All inhabitants of the earth will worship the beast—all whose names have not been written in the book of life belonging to the Lamb that was slain from the creation of the world. He who has an ear, let him hear. If anyone is to go into captivity, into captivity he will go. If anyone is to be killed with the sword, with the sword he will be killed. This calls for patient endurance and faithfulness on the part of the saints.

Revelation 13:1-10 (NIV)

In the next few sections we will learn how this dragon or system of evil works, and how it will flex its muscle tormenting those who follow the Lamb. We should hopefully begin to see the battle played out on earth! Once again, the sea is the place chaos or confusion comes. In the beginning of Genesis, God separates the dry land from chaos, water. The floodwaters in the story of Noah are the chaos of a world that does not recognize or trust God. The chaos waters of Egypt are separated so that the Israelites, the woman, could cross to the promise land. Through the waters of baptism the chaos of our lives are tamed.

Here our encounter with the first beast of Revelation also rises out of the sea, or the time of chaos. I will admit with most of the scholars at the time of John the beast was the Roman Empire. It has seven heads and ten horns like the dragon, but with ten crowns seemingly even more power than even the dragon. Power is the beast's very essence. The beast is power—seven heads, ten horns, ten crowns! The beast's power is that of governments whose influence is outreaching. Yes, it is the principle of political power, but it is more. The first beast can raise its ugly powerful head in any institution on earth, through state and local politics, secular organizations, and yes, even the church. Like I said, for John this political beast was the Roman Empire, but who is the beast today? Who is the beast today whose very essence is power?

In Paul's letter to the Roman people the apostle writes, "There is no authority except from God" (Romans 13:1, NRSV). It is God who created the institution of human government. It is the dragon who perverts what is already here. The dragon gives the authority to the institutional realm or the beast. So what God has instituted for our welfare is turned into an instrument of oppression and injustice by the beast. It is God's will there should be law and order. It is the dragon's work there is bad law, and disorder. The dragon puts blasphemies or lies in the mouth of the state so that it proclaims "I am god," and demands total unconditional allegiance. Even today in this country, we "pledge allegiance to the flag of the United States of America" and yet protest the fact she is under God. Times have not changed in the course of human history, and we see ever so clearly in the text where it talks about a "deadly wound that is healed." Here too we can go back in time and relate to a truth found in today's world. Notice the beast is bigger and more powerful than any single person. At the time of Christ, the emperors claimed to be divine. Domitian was to return to the throne after his death, perhaps not in the same person, but in the person of one of his successors. You see, there is a pattern that can be seen in the realm of politics and powerful institutions at any time in history through its government, state policies, liberal democracies, radical movements, dictatorship or communism all leading people to put their faith in this beast by the miracle of resurrection. The deadly wounded government, or institution, will rise up in a new place, in a new form at times of crisis continuing to convince humanity that our hope will be in the actions of the beast, blaspheming the name of God by not realizing that our only hope is not in human systems but in the slaughtered Lamb.

The church will suffer when it takes on the powers of this beast and criticizes its actions. All this will continue for forty-two months, the same three-and-a-half years the woman will exist in the wilderness. Throughout the history of the church, the beast from the sea will be active, and we as Christians will always have a dragon-influenced institution to contend with throughout our chaotic existence.

The Beastly Message

> Then I saw another beast that rose out of the earth; it had two horns like a lamb and it spoke like a dragon. It exercises all the authority of the

> first beast on its behalf, and it makes the earth and its inhabitants worship the first beast, whose mortal wound had been healed. It performs great signs, even making fire come down from heaven to earth in the sight of all; and by the signs that it is allowed to perform on behalf of the beast, it deceives the inhabitants of earth, telling them to make an image for the beast that had been wounded by the sword and yet lived; and it was allowed to give breath to the image of the beast so that the image of the beast could even speak and cause those who would not worship the image of the beast to be killed. Also it causes all, both small and great, both rich and poor, both free and slave, to be marked on the right hand or the forehead, so that no one can buy or sell who does not have the mark, that is, the name of the beast or the number of its name.
>
> Revelation 13:11-17 (NRSV)

Whatever it is, it looks like the Lamb and speaks like the dragon? It has the status of a prophet. It is concerned with worship and it appeals to the magical, all adding up to a type of message. However, it is a false message! In today's sense, the beast could include all of our ideology, our sense of morality, and our basic belief systems whether political, philosophical, or even religious. This second beast is anything that "gives breath' to a human social structure or institution organized independently of God. The point being, "organized independently of God."

While the first beast from the sea is Satan or the dragon's perversion of society through government and various institutions, the second beast rising from the earth perverts our moral base through its message. Therefore, the second beast is any false message, which in some way encourages undying devotion to the state, to political aspirations, even to religion, instead of the one seated upon the throne, and tries to do so by supernatural means. This evil message is so powerful it comes not only from institutions of government and state but false messages spill into and come out of the institution of the church. On our right, we have the conservative church working hand and hand with the state, amazing with political and patriotic crusades. On our left, we have those churches with their remarkable morality, the speaking of tongues, and sometimes spectacular healing attracting the uncommitted. Then we have all others, maybe not on the right or on the left, but still they promote the worship of the beast from the sea by proclaiming a gospel of prosperity, encouraging humankind to seek salvation in human achievement and human systems rather than in the grace of God and through the blood of the Lamb. The beast from the earth is any message that tries to make whatever "institution' so impressive that we commit our allegiance to the beast instead of to the slaughtered Lamb.

For those who are in the Spirit, those who are inhabitants of heaven, they are marked by the Lamb. For those who are inhabitants of the earth, or those who are deceived by this second beast, false ideas, false religion, they too are marked, but by the beast. They cannot survive without this crutch. The only salvation comes from the One who looks like a slaughtered

Lamb. All other promises, signs, and systems are simply the voice of the beast.

The Wisdom of 666

> This calls for wisdom: let anyone with understanding calculate the number of the beast, for it is the number of a person. Its number is six hundred sixty-six.
>
> Revelation 13:18 (NRSV)

What a great line in the Bible, huh? So what does 666 stand for? I believe this simple sentence is one of the most misunderstood lines of the entire Bible. Most people will say 666 is the sign of the devil, and I guess this might be okay, if we are willing to concede *we* just might be that devil. There have been scholars who say it was the sign of Nero or Domitian, emperors of the Roman Empire. This too could also have some merit, but if Revelation is a book about the past, present, and future, there have been rulers after Domitian and Nero who have been just as bad or worse. There have been all kinds of number combinations put together, volumes of books written all trying to figure out who or what is this 666, but we are looking in the wrong place. Remember it is a human number! The number does not stand for any particular person or particular institution or even the devil. The number simply stands for the beasts! And if one pays attention to the text we learn quite clearly it is a *human number!*

Before we examine 666, let's take a moment and look at some other strange human numbers. Jesus, in

Matthew 24:36, has already told us the length of time between his first and second coming is a matter known only to God, "Of that day and hour no one knows, not even the angels of heaven, nor the Son, but the Father only" (Matthew 24:36, NRSV). The actual number of years involved is divinely known, not humanly known. Nevertheless, to us human readers of Revelation, a number is given, a kind of a code, representing the length of the church's existence, or the return of Christ. The number could have been used because it is an appropriate "human number" closely corresponding to the length of Christ's ministry.

Another example of where I am going is the number of God's people. Again, in the Holy Scriptures, 2 Timothy 2:19, the text says the actual number of God's people is a divine secret, only "the Lord knows those who are his" (NRSV). If you recall when John is shown, the number was literally an innumerable multitude, but for the sake of us human readers, we are given something to chew on or imagine. So once again a number code is given, 144,000. Also another "good" number because it points our imagination in the right direction by joining together the twelve tribes of Israel multiplied by the twelve apostles, hopefully teaching we are all God's children.

With these examples in mind, it would be wrong to treat the number of the beasts as anything other than a "human number" symbolizing human institutions of bad government, and false messages. After all, the church is symbolized by pictures, the lampstands, the twenty-four elders, the woman, the great multitude, and a number of 144,000. The age of the church, or "end-times," are symbolized by pictures of the woman preserved in the wilderness, the two witnesses preaching, and also by a number or numbers—three-and-a-half years, forty-two months, 1260 days. Therefore, evil institutions and their false messages are symbolized by pictures; this time of a beast from the sea, a beast from the earth and now by a number, 666. A great number too! This calls for wisdom. *Let anyone with understanding calculate the number of the beast, for it is a human number.* Realize it is a number close to seven symbolizing wholeness or perfection but yet is not. Remember the beast looks like the Lamb, but not, and if the symbol of basic truth and wholeness is seven then six makes perfect sense for false messages and corrupt institutions. The beast in all of its activities is consistently and constantly missing the mark, so it's not just a single six but 666.

I'm sorry to take your devil in a little red suit away, but it has to be done. Otherwise, we will continue to miss the mark and blame the evils of the world, the work of the dragon on the devil, on others, or worse yet, on God. However, blaming evil and the suffering of the world on the devil, on others, and on God has been our calling card since the beginning. Somehow, the cycle needs to broken. Somehow, we need a new starting point and perhaps this strange book is capable of doing just that!

Understand in the beginning, everything God created was good, not perfect mind you but very good. God then created human beings. The Christian faith, Jewish faith, and Islamic faith all teach that God did something special by breathing into you and I the

Spirit, the breath of God, making you and I in His image. At this moment whenever that may be, we as human beings begin to ask what I call the "depth" questions. Who am I? Who created all of this? What is my purpose? Without those questions, we are really no different than an anteater. God answers those questions by responding to our hearts and minds saying, "I created you and all that you see and don't see. I give to you the world on a silver platter, and all I ask is that you take care of my creation, including one another. You are free, free to question and search all your little hearts desire. I only ask of you one more thing. See the tree in the middle of the garden? That is the tree of knowledge. Leave that one single tree alone. Okay?" But it is not okay! We desire more! We desire the infinite knowledge of God, or better put, we think we desire the infinite knowledge of God. I'm not quite certain we could deal with that burden. Anyway, we reach out our hands daily and eat, not trusting that the One who sits on the Throne has our best interest at heart. However, if you remember the creation story, what happens next? After we have eaten the forbidden fruit God asks, "What have you done?" We reply, "The devil made me do it!" Worse yet we blame God or others by saying, "The woman *you* gave me—she made me do it!"

So, you bet! There is an evil power stronger than anyone can defeat or destroy. But who has created this evil one? Not God! Everything God created is very good. So who has created this power of evil? We have! Our original sin, or originating sin of not trusting God's knowledge grows and grows into a system of evil gaining strength and power as time goes on, actually to the point where the dragon of evil, the beast of the sea, the beast of the earth take on a life of their own, and it now becomes absolutely impossible to escape their influence. Think for a moment about your children born into a world where racism and sexism are the messages of the institution from birth. We are dying from cancer at an alarming rate because of what we as co-creators have done to air, water, and ground. Young people are committing suicide and dying in our rehab centers, on our highways due to drunk drivers because we, as a society, have become cold and immune to the problem of drug addiction in the world. Our kids are being shot and killed in our schools because we, as a society, have put guns in the hands of those who desire violence, leading to a crime rate spiraling out of control. We have created an institution or system that allows millions and millions of children to starve, while 10 percent of the earth's population could feed those millions, if only they were willing to give up a little of the caviar and champagne. The society, as a whole, has become so interested in money, status, and power that young people have no choice but to grow up thinking and believing these two beasts are their gods! The evil is unleashed in the world through the continuous abuse of our human freedom, and believe you me, this evil dragon does acquire a real life of its own! Your children are born into this sinful situation—a situation co-created by us and our ancestors, not by God! Until we are willing to trust God and accept the blame of eating the forbidden fruit matters will continue to get worse and the sphere of sin will continue to grow and grow, gaining more and more power. Folks this is not something called the devil, or some stupid number, but something called human beings. Remember the text says, "This calls for wisdom; let anyone with understanding calculate the number of the beast, for it is the number of a person. Its number is 666."

The Kingdom of God

> Then I looked, and there before me was the Lamb, standing on Mount Zion, and with him 144,000 who had his name and his Father's name written on their foreheads. And I heard a sound from heaven like the roar of rushing waters and like a loud peal of thunder. The sound I heard was like that of harpists playing their harps. And they sang a new song before the throne and before the four living creatures and the elders. No one could learn the song except the 144,000 who had been redeemed from the earth. These are those who did not defile themselves with women, for they kept themselves pure. They follow the Lamb wherever he goes. They were purchased from among men and offered as first fruits to God and the Lamb. No lie was found in their mouths; they are blameless.
>
> Revelation 14:1-5 (NIV)

While the situation looks bleak, there are alternatives to the beast from the sea and the beast from the earth. The counterpart of a worldly institution would be a godly kingdom. Here we get a glimpse of that godly institution where one sees an alternative type of praise, let me repeat, an alternative type of praise. Praise to God, not to the beasts or the dragon. However, the only ones included come from the great multitude or the 144,000—those who have washed their robes with the blood of the Lamb. Like the text says, only those who have never had sex are included! I'm just kidding! I wanted to see if you were still awake. Yet see how ridiculous that statement sounds if one takes Scripture literally? Of course, the book is not talking about virginity in the sense of having sex, or being celibate. The Bible commends the institution of marriage. Yes, many of the early Christians interpreted this short passage a warning against sexual intercourse and even marriage. Sure if one searches the Bible, one will find constant warnings about virginity in the Old Testament, but it is in reference to faithfulness to God, not sex. Throughout the prophets, Israel is accused of sleeping around, sleeping around with other gods and not being faithful to Yahweh. The virginity refers to those who have not defiled themselves with other loves, better yet, not had a loving relationship with the beasts. These are the ones who will be redeemed. Through the slaughter of the Lamb and through his blood shed on a cross you have been redeemed/paid for/bought back. Redemption is once again that new starting point needed! It is the loving action of God making you blameless through the Lamb's forgiveness. Your robe has now been washed in the blood of the Lamb. To you it is a free gift! It cost God everything! Our only response can and should be that of praise, always remembering those whose worship the One on the Throne and Lamb take on a new lifestyle. Can you learn the song?

The Message of the Lamb

Then I saw another angel flying in midheaven, with an eternal gospel to proclaim to those who live on the earth to every nation and tribe and language and people. He said in a loud voice, "Fear God and give him glory, for the hour of his judgment has come; and worship him who made heaven and earth, the sea and the springs of water." Then another angel, a second, followed, saying, "Fallen, fallen is Babylon the great! She has made all nations drink of the wine of the wrath of her fornication." Then another angel, a third, followed them, crying with a loud voice, "Those who worship the beast and its image, and receive a mark on their foreheads or on their hands, they will also drink the wine of God's wrath, poured unmixed into the cup of his anger, and they will be tormented with fire and sulfur in the presence of the holy angels and in the presence of the Lamb. And the smoke of their torment goes up forever and ever. There is no rest day or night for those who worship the beast and its image and for anyone who receives the mark of its name." Here is a call for the endurance of the saints, those who keep the commandments of God and hold fast to the faith of Jesus. And I heard a voice from heaven saying, "Write this: Blessed are the dead who from now on die in the Lord." "Yes," says the Spirit, "they will rest from their labors, for their deeds follow them."

Revelation 14:6-13 (NRSV)

It's not rocket science! The opening visions showed that much of the world is governed or ruled by the

Dragon/Satan/Evil, and I doubt there is a soul who would argue the point. The first vision shows human institutions, be it government, social organizations, even religious institutions of the first beast born out of chaos or confusion. The second vision shows us a beast rising up from the earth with the false message the institutions spew forth, causing the world to pledge their allegiance to the first beast. The third vision showed the opposite of the first, in which we saw the members of a godly society, the 144,000, instead of a beastly society. Therefore, we should assume the fourth vision will show once again the opposite of the second with its evil message. Instead of now believing what the institution and certain religions proclaim we see and hear a Holy Word given to us from three angels, or messengers, and their message is threefold.

The first angel's message is the basic good news of how to be in a right relationship with God. It is the eternal gospel! This good news is summarized by recognizing God and Creator and Judge, the beginning and end of your existence, and all will be well! "Fear God and give Him glory" (Revelation 14:7, NRSV). The fear of God is different than we might normally think. In the Bible, fear means a type of respect or reverence, afraid to disappoint the One on the Throne. Yet all is not well, because we do not recognize God as Creator and Judge and give God the honor and respect that is deserved. We do not take care of God's creation and everything in it. So the second angel also has a message. It is the spirit of Babylon that has infected all nations and made human beings incapable of responding to the first angel's gospel, but even for all her power, Babylon is doomed to destruction.

Here we are introduced to another fascinating symbol. Remember, how I have mentioned a few times that the Bible is a wonderful teacher and how the book of Revelation will show various symbols and pictures representing the same things. Babylon is now simply another picture of the beast from the sea, the worldly institutions, or government in rebellion against God and the first angel's gospel. Babylon will have an entire scene to herself, and I will deal more with her later, but right now simply remember she is doomed, because she lures us away from where our praise and glory should be—to God and the slaughtered Lamb!

Finally, the third angel brings us a personal challenge. The ones who identify with the Babylon/the beast will share in her fate and will "drink the wine of God's wrath." Those however, who identify with Christ will endure forever and ever. Over and over again, Revelation points out the situation, gives you a choice, and then shows you the result of your decision.

The Harvest of the Lamb

> Then I looked, and there was a white cloud, and seated on the cloud was one like the Son of Man, with a golden crown on his head, and a sharp sickle in his hand! Another angel came out of the temple, calling with a loud voice to the one who sat on the cloud, "Use your sickle and reap, for the hour to reap has come, because the harvest of the earth is fully ripe." So the one who sat on the cloud swung his sickle over the earth, and the earth was reaped.

> Then another angel came out of the temple in heaven, and he too had a sharp sickle. Then another angel came out from the altar, the angel who has authority over fire, and he called with a loud voice to him who had the sharp sickle, "Use your sharp sickle and gather the clusters of the vine of the earth, for its grapes are ripe." So the angel swung his sickle over the earth and gathered the vintage of the earth, and he threw it into the great wine press of the wrath of God. And the wine press was trodden outside the city, and blood flowed from the wine press, as high as a horse's bridle, for a distance of about two hundred miles.
>
> Revelation 14:14-20 (NRSV)

Has your robe been washed in the blood of the Lamb? I hope so, because the grape harvest destined for the wine press of God's wrath producing a tide of blood is yet another symbol of the end times. The reaping of the wicked are the results of their choice to follow the two beasts. The land will be a blood bath from end to end, 1,600 stadia, which is two hundred miles, and by no coincidence the length of the holy lands. However, these two reapers must wait for the word of God before they begin their harvest and only God knows the time or the hour. For three-and-a-half years, there will be conflict between the beasts and its message and the church and its gospel. In the end, there will be a final reaping. For as long as the church exists, these four powers will be locked in constant battle. Revelation is not so much a book pointing to the future but revealing past events continuing into today and will continue tomorrow.

So let's recap this difficult yet truthful chapter. It's very important we understand the characters of this vision so the book may come alive and bring us its promised blessing. Remember, it does call for wisdom! In one corner, we have the powerful institution of government or organizations of any kind, including religious, or better yet the "system' of the first beast, humankind organized socially and politically as the dragon/evil wants it to be, not what it should be, with power structures at any particular time serving its selfish needs. Next to it, on the same side we have the second beast, powerful ideologies, our belief system, the message, which we use to justify the actions of the system. Over against these two powerhouses are the Kingdom of God, a "holy' nation, the church (when it is pure), God's redeemed society, the lampstands, the woman, Israel, the 144,000, the great multitude, a different type of "system"—a system not based on the logic of our minds, but on the grace of our creator and judge. Finally, in the fourth corner and opposite our human beliefs and false religions, which give the dragon life is the gospel of truth that comes from the church of God, the gospel of the Christian faith summarized as a message of grace and of warning—like a sharp two edge sword. Trust God and take care of creation—including each other! Every single event in history can be seen as part of the conflict between these four forces, two on one side and two on the other, with completely opposite messages coming from completely opposite societies.

What Are the Seven Plagues?

Then I saw another portent in heaven, great and amazing: seven angels with seven plagues, which are the last, for with them the wrath of God is ended. And I saw what appeared to be a sea of glass mixed with fire, and those who had conquered the beast and its image and the number of its name, standing beside the sea of glass with harps of God in their hands. And they sing the song of Moses, the servant of God, and the song of the Lamb: "Great and amazing are your deeds, Lord God the Almighty! Just and true are your ways, King of the nations! Lord, who will not fear and glorify your name? For you alone are holy. All nations will come and worship before you, for your judgments have been revealed." After this I looked, and the temple of the tent of witness in heaven was opened, and out of the temple came the seven angels with the seven plagues, robed in pure bright linen, with golden sashes across their chests. Then one of the four living creatures gave the seven angels seven golden bowls full of the wrath of God, who lives forever and ever; and the temple was filled with smoke from the glory of God and from his power, and no one could enter the temple until the seven plagues of the seven angels were ended.

Then I heard a loud voice from the temple telling the seven angels, "Go and pour out on the earth the seven bowls of the wrath of God."

Revelation 15:1-16:1 (NRSV)

As we read aloud, notice the sequence of John's visions is not laid out in a chronological order. Yet the scenes are unified in a subtle manner. The first section of the book addresses the church in the world. The second part points to the suffering of the world and the church. Section three brings out the trumpets warning the world. The fourth scene teaches about the conflicts on earth between the two beasts, the church and its message, ending with the assurance that God is in control and will not allow this struggle to continue forever. God will act when the harvest is ripe. God is a God of mercy and grace, but also a God who will punish evil. It is now that time for "God to pour out on the earth the seven bowls of the wrath of God" (Revelation 16:1, NRSV).

In this next section, we will see that the holiness of God can be a terrible thing. Fear will take over this entire scene. We have been told the situation, the warnings have been given and our options explained. Now we see the angel's bowls filled with the wrath of God who lives forever and ever. You do remember wrath? Wrath is not the cruelty of God but the kindness of God. Strange, huh? God's wrath is not directly caused by God, but by us refusing to worship the only One who deserves our praise; God and the Lamb. Folks, we ourselves bring on God's wrath and these punishments are sevenfold because they are full and complete. I'm not quite certain why we don't like to read these passages because notice one thing right off the bat, for the one who worships the Lamb, these horrible bowls will not play a part in their lives according to the text. Let me repeat, all who have not been sealed as followers of the Lamb will suffer, however, the inhabitants of heaven, the woman, the church, the lamp stands, the 144,000, the great multitude will not experience this horrible scene. Once again, always asking is your robe washed in the blood of the Lamb? I hope so, because the partial troubles we experienced in God's warnings to the world are nothing compared to the bowls. The bowls are a final earthly punishment!

The song of Moses and the song of the Lamb are the same song, bringing together the old and new, Hebrew and Christian. The song referenced begins like this, "The Lord is my strength and my might, and he has become my salvation; this is my God, and I will praise him" (Exodus 15:1, NRSV). It goes on and tells the story through the centuries how God conquered Egypt and saved Israel. Through the years that followed, God's people celebrated the deliverance by the annual death of the Passover lamb, and in the fullness of time there follows a greater Lamb, Jesus. Now the real Egypt is destroyed and the real Israel is saved. Like I said, the song of Moses and song of the Lamb are the same song.

Remember the prayers of the saints for justice? They are now being answered, again. One thing that I find interesting is the bowls are first given to the angels by one of the four living creatures, or the representatives of nature. In the end, God will arm creation to punish evil. Even nature, knowing that it will suffer when the plagues come, is willing to obey the Lord of nature. In all the gospels, Jesus calms the sea and the wind. Even the sea and wind obey! Even nature obeys! Too bad we can't or won't.

The throne of the beast has invaded our society, a society planned by God and perverted by our following the dragon and the two beasts without reference to the Lamb. Now this throne will be covered by darkness. If you think things are bad now, just wait. There will be utter chaos in an already confused society. The godless throne that rose up against the church will now pay and pay dearly.

THE FIRST SIX PLAGUES

> So the first angel went and poured his bowl on the earth, and a foul and painful sore came on those who had the mark of the beast and who worshiped its image. The second angel poured his bowl into the sea, and it became like the blood of a corpse, and every living thing in the sea died. The third angel poured his bowl into the rivers and the springs of water, and they became blood.

> And I heard the angel of the waters say, "You are just, O Holy One, who are and were, for you have judged these things; because they shed the blood of saints and prophets, you have given them blood to drink. It is what they deserve!" And I heard the altar respond, "Yes, O Lord God, the Almighty, your judgments are true and just!" The fourth angel poured his bowl on the sun, and it was allowed to scorch people with fire; they were scorched by the fierce heat, but they cursed the name of God, who had authority over these plagues, and they did not repent and give him glory. The fifth angel poured his bowl on the throne of the beast, and its kingdom was plunged into darkness; people gnawed their tongues in agony, and cursed the God of heaven because of their pains and sores, and they did not repent of their deeds. The sixth angel poured his bowl on the great river Euphrates, and its water was dried up in order to prepare the way for the kings from the east. And I saw three foul spirits like frogs coming from the mouth of the dragon, from the mouth of the beast, and from the mouth of the false prophet. These are demonic spirits, performing signs, who go abroad to the kings of the whole world, to assemble them for battle on the great day of God the Almighty.
>
> Revelation 16:2-14 (NRSV)

The warnings have been given and now it is time to say good-bye. I hope these visions upset each and every one of us, because they will affect all those who place their trust in the worldly institutions and its message, and I don't know about you, but I pray I will not be part of this scene. The first four bowls of plagues or punishments closely resemble the first four trumpets of warnings, each affecting the earth, the sea, the rivers, and springs of water, and finally the air or our environment. Yet even here, the ones who have heard the warnings and experienced the plagues still do not give praise and honor to the Creator. The text says, "They cursed the name of God and did not repent." We are a stubborn lot! So the fifth angel attacks what we hold most dear, the institution, throwing the world into darkness with nothing left to rely upon.

The sixth angel prepares us for the last battle, Armageddon, another fabulous picture for the end times. While the Euphrates is known as a place life comes from in Genesis, the first book of the Bible, now the Euphrates becomes the place where death comes from in Revelation, the last book of the Bible. The dragon is evil. The first beast is the godless society, or the world, our manner of government. The false prophet now introduced is the same as the second beast, our ideology, morals, giving us yet another symbol or picture to toy with. They are gathered now together for one last stand against the unstoppable power of God Almighty. Armageddon is the end! The catch word, Armageddon itself, means "hill of Megiddo," an actual site a few miles from the modern city of Haifa in Israel overlooking the crossing place of some of the most important routes of the ancient world, sometimes called the "crossroad of the Middle East." At this site many crucial and bloody battles of history have been fought, making it an appropriate symbol for the final battle, the last stage of the divine punishment. It is where God and the forces of evil will converge for one last battle. Having seen the perversion of human society placed in confusion and darkness the dragon now says, "If I can no longer influence and pervert, I will destroy," so the dragon and the two beasts set out on a killing frenzy, maybe not at this exact location but wherever it occurs, it will be the most crucial and bloodiest battle of all.

The Seventh Plague

> ("See, I am coming like a thief! Blessed is the one who stays awake and is clothed, not going about naked and exposed to shame.") And they assembled them at the place that in Hebrew is called Harmagedon. The seventh angel poured his bowl into the air, and a loud voice came out of the temple, from the throne, saying, "It is done!" And there came flashes of lightning, rumblings, peals of thunder, and a violent earthquake, such as had not occurred since people were upon the earth, so violent was that earthquake. The great city was split into three parts, and the cities of the nations fell. God remembered great Babylon and gave her the wine-cup of the fury of his wrath. And every island fled away, and no mountains were to be found; and huge hailstones, each weighing about a hundred pounds, dropped from heaven on people, until they cursed God for the plague of the hail, so fearful was that plague.
>
> Revelation 16:15-21 (NRSV)

So while trumpet six was the last warning bringing death before them to see, bowl seven will be the last punishment bringing death for them to feel. God's job title is to bring justice. Satan's job title is deception.

The two of them come together at the crossroads of Armageddon. Yet inside the description of the end of the world lies a hidden meaning. "See, I am coming like a thief! Blessed is the one who stays awake and is clothed, not going about naked and exposed to shame" (Revelation 16:15, NRSV).

I'm not so sure any of us will actually see the day of Armageddon as the end of the world, but tucked away in the middle of the scene is a personal warning. Each of you will have your own Armageddon where the forces of good and evil, the forces of life and death will be fought. None of us know when our life will end, it will come like a thief, and we will stand before the judgment of God. Blessed is the one who is awake!

Even in the end with the seventh plague, God's presence is still evident with the lightning, voices, thunder, and earthquake. The pouring out of bowl seven will sweep away time and history, replaced by eternity with God. When that day comes, not only will civilizations collapse, the mountains and islands will vanish. When the great day of God Almighty comes, the powers of this world will find themselves suddenly confronted by a rejected Lamb.

Who Is the Whore of Babylon?

Then one of the seven angels who had the seven bowls came and said to me, "Come, I will show you the judgment of the great whore who is seated on many waters, with whom the kings of the earth have committed fornication, and with the wine of whose fornication the inhabitants of the earth have become drunk." So he carried me away in the spirit into a wilderness, and I saw a woman sitting on a scarlet beast that was full of blasphemous names, and it had seven heads and ten horns. The woman was clothed in purple and scarlet, and adorned with gold and jewels and pearls, holding in her hand a golden cup full of abominations and the impurities of her fornication; and on her forehead was written a name, a mystery: "Babylon the great, mother of

> whores and of earth's abominations." And I saw that the woman was drunk with the blood of the saints and the blood of the witnesses to Jesus. When I saw her, I was greatly amazed.
>
> Revelation 17:1-6 (NRSV)

Each revelation has been more awesome than the last and this lengthy section is loaded with great truth. We have already been introduced to the dragon and two beasts. Now we will see the realities about these ever present and real evils told in yet another manner, another picture: Babylon the whore! She has appeared on two previous occasions and in both of those cases we learned Babylon was simply another picture of what I called the ideology of evil, false messages of the second beast, lifting up the dragon's godless society to a position of supreme authority, opposed by the divine ideology, the everlasting gospel of trusting God and taking care of creation. But who is she? John says at the end of this section, "When I saw her I was greatly amazed." You see, it would be very foolish to underestimate her. Even John finds himself marveling. However, he has been taken into a wilderness in order to witness this scene and while the wilderness represents many things in the Bible, it is basically a form of separation from the affairs of civilization. John can now see things as they really are in the wilderness.

Yes, she is a woman to behold, but underneath all the glamour she is simply "the great whore," with fornication, fornication, fornication written all over her, seducing humankind away from its purpose in life, tempting them like that great serpent of the garden of

Eden. John uses the word fornication three different times and this lovely word comes from the Greek root, porn! Yet remember, we are not talking about sexual immorality. We are talking about an immorality much deeper, unfaithfulness to the Almighty. Later in the next section, we discover the counterpart to Babylon the whore is Jerusalem the bride. Trying to teach it is a faithful bond of marriage being the goal of our relationship with God. But right now, right here good ole Babylon the whore seduces the inhabitants of the earth and we end up sleeping with the whore instead of God. We see her strength and her power. She is sitting atop a scarlet beast with seven heads of authority and ten horns of strength reminding us of the same seven heads and tens horns of the dragon, giving her and her beast enormous influence. She is drunk in her apparent victory over those who witness to the Christian truth she hates. "When I saw her, I marveled greatly."

The Mystery of the Whore

> But the angel said to me, "Why are you so amazed? I will tell you the mystery of the woman, and of the beast with seven heads and ten horns that carries her. The beast that you saw was, and is not, and is about to ascend from the bottomless pit and go to destruction. And the inhabitants of the earth, whose names have not been written in the book of life from the foundation of the world, will be amazed when they see the beast, because it was and is not and is to come."
>
> Revelation 17:7-8 (NRSV)

However, the angel will now tell John the mystery. Finally, we'll get to the bottom of this! Yes, the angel will explain, but on the surface, it doesn't seem that he does a very good job. Mystery here does not carry its normal modern definition, at least not in such a way that you can follow a series of clues and solve the puzzle. We have many of these mysteries within the Christian faith presenting obstacles for some trying to find meaning. Did you know for example that the word *sacrament* is actually a Greek root word carrying the literal meaning of "mystery"? In my tradition, there are two of these so-called mysteries or sacraments: holy baptism and holy communion. In baptism, common water is used, and in communion, simple bread and wine are offered. Yet coming through these common simple elements, combined with God's Word of promise we have access to the real presence of the slaughtered Lamb offering strength, comfort, forgiveness of sin, and eternal life. So how in the world does one explain these chief elements of the Christian faith? You can't! It is a mystery! It is rather a truth that you either know or do not know depending on whether it has been revealed by God. Yet it has been revealed to you! The mystery is a truth hidden from some but "has now been revealed to his holy apostles," and they reveal it to us through the little scroll—the gospel of Christ Jesus.

Instead of giving us impossible clues to solve the puzzle, the angel will show us the real meaning once again, as always through a picture. It is a mystery, a mystery of the whore and the beasts. We cannot separate them. Yes, she is equivalent of the second beast of the earth, representing false messages or any ideas that teach our salvation and future are based on human efforts and ideas, but she is now riding or combined with the beast from the sea representing human society, our form of government without God. The first beast is sort of the institution, while the second is sort of the message. Here the whore and the scarlet beast form a single mystery. *They are the mystery of culture!* She becomes how we identify ourselves, not as creatures of the one on the throne but as followers of the whore. She is to be regarded as one truth, combining the beasts to give us yet another powerful picture or symbol. The power of the organization combined with the elements of its message over a long period of time end up actually defining who we are. We are identified by, for lack of a better word, our culture—a way of life for an entire society, including art, dress, language, manners, ritual, and religion. The whore and the scarlet beast actually form our culture. In John's day, it would have been the Roman culture. In Moses' day, the Egyptian culture. In our day, it is the culture of the western world. So you see, just like John, you are not going to learn of its meaning by having it explained to you but by having your mind focused on the vision and in several different ways.

Yet hidden in the midst of this passage, we find one sentence I find extremely exciting. Notice something very important about the whore and the beast that carries her. These forces of evil—the godless institution and its message defining who we are— are referred to three times as "it was, *and is not*, and is to come." There is a very subtle difference between the beasts and the whore and the Lamb. Remember in the very beginning of Revelation, the one sitting on the throne and the Lamb are referred to as the one "who was, who is, and who is to come." Here now the woman and the beast are not!

Evil has been around since our existence and it will continue, but pay attention; evil does not have to be in our lives here and now! It is not! It was, it is to come, *but it is not*! Evil, the beasts, and the whore are realities of the past and realities of the future, but are not a reality of the present. If you open up to the Lamb and the message of the gospel, the one seated on the throne *is* a force in your life *today*, and the beast and the whore *are not*! How true, huh? Evil has been a part of my life in the past. Evil will be part of my life in the future. But it does not have to be right now! This calls for a mind with wisdom! Can we begin to place our trust in the mysteries of God where through baptism we are marked with the seal of God and named as children of the Most High? Can we begin to place our trust in the mystery of Holy Communion where we are washed clean through the blood of the Lamb? If so, we have come to that fresh start, where right now at this moment the whore does not have to be part of our life and we can now begin to trust in the wonderful promises of one seated upon the throne. After all, as far as I know, God has not lied to us yet!

The Wisdom of the Seven Heads and Seven Hills

"This calls for a mind that has wisdom: the seven heads are seven mountains on which the woman is seated; also, they are seven kings, of whom five have fallen, one is living, and the other has not yet come; and when he comes, he must remain only a little while. As for the beast that was and is not, it is an eighth but it belongs to the seven, and it goes to destruction. And the ten horns that you saw are ten kings who have not yet received a kingdom, but they are to receive authority as kings for one hour, together with the beast. These are united in yielding their power and authority to the beast; they will make war on the Lamb, and the Lamb will conquer them, for he is Lord of lords and King of kings, and those with him are called and chosen and faithful."

Revelation 17:9-14 (NRSV)

Many of the commentaries make such a big deal out of the seven heads and the seven mountains or hills that Rome is built upon, and yes, their interpretation makes the passage very real to those reading it two thousand years ago. It does relate to the Roman Empire and its message, but we need to look to its innermost truth, or another mystery. The fact that Rome is built on seven hills is not irrelevant, but it stops short of the mystery. I have mentioned a few times that John's vision is a type of summary of the entire Bible. It is enhanced by visions from Daniel, Ezekiel, Jeremiah, Isaiah, and others. In these Hebrew visions, we also see pictures of evil empires and godless societies, or cultures that have dominated the lives and existence of many, and if one traced these empires of biblical history, one finds that Egypt is the first, Assyria the second, Babylon, Persia, then Rome, and whatever follows Rome would be the sixth. Okay? Stay with me here!

The mystical meaning of the sevenfold king is its vast influence in our lives. Since the number seven is complete or whole, then any Christian of any century should be able to look back and count five previous worldly governments with its message creating culture. The text teaches that those five have fallen and the sixth is the one we know to be in power today. Meaning the USA would now be the "one who is." Yet, sad but true, it will remain only a little while and another, the seventh, will take over, but according to the text, it too will be like the rest and go to destruction. This is the way it will be the whole of our existence! We always think there will be a heavenly kingdom on earth better than the last. We can fix it! We can make it better than any of the previous governments, or as the text claims, an eighth one, even better than the whole. But no, whatever comes next is simply part of the seven destined to fall because we worship the dragon, the whore and its beast, and not the slaughtered Lamb. The process will continue throughout history—one king replacing the next, one government replacing the last, one culture springing up anew, all with heads of the beast. These future kings will hold power for a very short time in the scheme of things, an hour as compared to 1260 days.

A Split in the Ranks of Evil

> And he said to me, "The waters that you saw, where the whore is seated, are peoples and multitudes

and nations and languages. And the ten horns that you saw, they and the beast will hate the whore; they will make her desolate and naked; they will devour her flesh and burn her up with fire. For God has put it into their hearts to carry out his purpose by agreeing to give their kingdom to the beast, until the words of God will be fulfilled. The woman you saw is the great city that rules over the kings of the earth."

After this I saw another angel coming down from heaven, having great authority; and the earth was made bright with his splendor. He called out with a mighty voice, "Fallen, fallen is Babylon the great! It has become a dwelling place of demons, a haunt of every foul spirit, a haunt of every foul bird, a haunt of every foul and hateful beast. For all the nations have drunk of the wine of the wrath of her fornication, and the kings of the earth have committed fornication with her, and the merchants of the earth have grown rich from the power of her luxury."

Revelation 17:15-18:3 (NRSV)

At the end of the forty-two months, we are given a glimpse into the future with a split in the ranks of evil. The beast's ten horns turn against the woman and destroy her. Evil rising up against evil for a short period will cause all hell to break loose promoting now the beast's cause with brute force. Jesus touches on this mystery in the gospels where he talks about Satan rising up against Satan. Think about what happens among all the revolutionaries? They will eventually turn to blood. Human history of Satanic governments begin with sometimes good intentions, human ideals of grandeur but eventually the ideals and belief systems are replaced by the government itself and in turn dominate even those with the notion that we can make things work. We cannot, at least not without the Lamb.

In the last days, the dragon's power will be made known for what it is, and the beast will turn on its former ally, the woman, discarding ideas and beliefs, now relying on naked power. Even though the two comprise the single work of the dragon, it will not be long till the beast or the institution will no longer need or heed to the ideology of the whore. The whore is enthroned on the beast, the beast on many waters, but the beast will turn and take over. We may think our institution and its message creates the perfect culture, but in the end, you just read what will happen.

The angel seems to dig through the dictionary in order to find the appropriate words that apply to the beast's strength and evil, because in daily life the pearls and golden cup have an extreme fascination. The world is powerful and its message is attractive! We become drunk with visions of becoming rich and powerful. That is why the spell needs to be broken by a voice of even greater authority. "Fallen, fallen is Babylon the great!" The second angel comes from heaven and assures us of her downfall, warning us about putting our trust in her. Whether it is capitalism or communism, whether it is power and riches, we need to be reminded and warned that neither the beasts nor the whore is permanently in power, despite all the symbolism of the everlasting hills and strength. One day it will fall! One day it will fall and then where will we put our trust and gain true wealth?

The Fall of Babylon the Whore

Then I heard another voice from heaven saying, "Come out of her, my people, so that you do not take part in her sins, and so that you do not share in her plagues; for her sins are heaped high as heaven, and God has remembered her iniquities. Render to her as she herself has rendered, and repay her double for her deeds; mix a double draught for her in the cup she mixed. As she glorified herself and lived luxuriously, so give her a like measure of torment and grief. Since in her heart she says, 'I rule as a queen; I am no widow, and I will never see grief,' therefore her plagues will come in a single day pestilence and mourning and famine and she will be burned with fire; for mighty is the Lord God who judges her." And the kings of the earth, who committed fornication and lived in luxury with her, will weep and wail over her when they see the smoke of her burning; they will stand far off, in fear of her torment, and say, "Alas, alas, the great city, Babylon, the mighty city! For in one hour your judgment has come." And the merchants of the earth weep and mourn for her, since no one buys their cargo anymore, cargo of gold, silver, jewels and pearls, fine linen, purple, silk and scarlet, all kinds of scented wood, all articles of ivory, all articles of costly wood, bronze, iron, and marble, cinnamon, spice, incense, myrrh, frankincense, wine, olive oil, choice flour and wheat, cattle and sheep, horses and chariots, slaves and human lives. "The fruit for which your soul longed has gone from you, and all your dainties and your splendor are lost to you, never to be found again!" The merchants of these wares, who gained wealth from her, will stand far off, in fear of her torment, weeping and mourning aloud, "Alas, alas, the great city, clothed in fine linen, in purple and scarlet, adorned with gold, with jewels, and with pearls! For in one hour all this wealth has been laid waste!" And all shipmasters and seafarers, sailors and all whose trade is on the sea, stood far off and cried out as they saw the smoke of her burning, "What city was like the great city?" And they threw dust on their heads, as they wept and mourned, crying out, "Alas, alas, the great city, where all who had ships at sea grew rich by her wealth! For in one hour she has been laid waste. Rejoice over her, O heaven, you saints and apostles and prophets! For God has given judgment for you against her."

Revelation 18:4-20 (NRSV)

Yes, the mystical Babylon with all of her pride and luxury intoxicates the nations. However, because of her wickedness, she will be punished, and we see the results with the suddenness of her fiery destruction. We see the horror of those who have come to depend on her and the warning that God's people not be involved. The end of this particular king or godless culture is a truth we all must recognize. It is the downfall of every single civilization that does not place their trust in the One seated on the throne and the Lamb's message. In what direction are we heading?

Silence

> Then a mighty angel took up a stone like a great millstone and threw it into the sea, saying, "With such violence Babylon the great city will be thrown down, and will be found no more; and the sound of harpists and minstrels and of flutists and trumpeters will be heard in you no more; and an artisan of any trade will be found in you no more; and the sound of the millstone will be heard in you no more; and the light of a lamp will shine in you no more; and the voice of bridegroom and bride will be heard in you no more; for your merchants were the magnates of the earth, and all nations were deceived by your sorcery. And in you was found the blood of prophets and of saints, and of all who have been slaughtered on earth."
>
> Revelation 18:24 (NRSV)

I think it's rather odd, in a book where destruction is usually announced by loud noises, that here there is silence. No more sounds of playing, no more sounds of industry. The lamps of the city of Babylon go out, and stillness falls upon it. The stone sinks beneath the surface, and civilization as we know it ceases, as if it had never been. That's how quick it will happen, like a stone thrown into the sea of chaos.

Who Is the Bride of the Lamb?

After this I heard what seemed to be the loud voice of a great multitude in heaven, saying, "Hallelujah! Salvation and glory and power to our God, for his judgments are true and just; he has judged the great whore who corrupted the earth with her fornication, and he has avenged on her the blood of his servants." Once more they said, "Hallelujah! The smoke goes up from her forever and ever." And the twenty-four elders and the four living creatures fell down and worshiped God who is seated on the throne, saying, "Amen. Hallelujah!" And from the throne came a voice saying, "Praise our God, all you his servants, and all who fear him, small and great." Then I heard what seemed to be the voice of a great multitude, like the sound of many waters and like the sound of

> mighty thunderpeals, crying out, "Hallelujah! For the Lord our God the Almighty reigns. Let us rejoice and exult and give him the glory, for the marriage of the Lamb has come, and his bride has made herself ready; to her it has been granted to be clothed with fine linen, bright and pure"— for the fine linen is the righteous deeds of the saints. And the angel said to me, "Write this: Blessed are those who are invited to the marriage supper of the Lamb." And he said to me, "These are true words of God." Then I fell down at his feet to worship him, but he said to me, "You must not do that! I am a fellow servant with you and your comrades who hold the testimony of Jesus. Worship God! For the testimony of Jesus is the spirit of prophecy."
>
> Revelation 19:1-10 (NRSV)

Now after the whore we find the bride. Brilliant, huh? The bride, or the church, is the counterpart of the whore of Babylon. Recall at the beginning of the book those who worship take on a different lifestyle than what culture teaches. The magnificent and complex descriptions of the whore have been presented in elaborate detail, but the wedding dress of the bride is plain and simple: "fine linen, bright, and pure." The text tells us the fine linen is our works performed to the glory of God, and these will be the ones invited to the marriage supper of the Lamb. Don't believe me? "These are true words of God" (Revelation 19:9, NRSV). Revelation will ever so slowly begin to tie the loose ends together. Earlier we witnessed the prayers of the saints rising up before God asking for justice, and now we find the twenty-four elders—the twelve tribes of Israel and the twelve apostles—representing all God's people, along with all of nature once again worshiping at the throne of God because justice has been served. We have seen the work of the dragon setting about the project of destroying God's servants. The work comes powerfully as an institution promising the way, and a message presenting evil in the same manner the serpent offered the fruit in the garden of Eden—good for food, a delight to the eyes and desired to make one wise. The mouthpiece of this satanic message is Babylon the whore, our culture, but from above God reaches down with salvation both for his church and for the world, with glory and power more than that of Babylon.

The revelation has been so overwhelming that John falls down to worship at the angel's feet, but the angel will have none of this and wants John to realize that both of them stand on the same level as servants of God. The same applies to each of us. Yes, it is true that the angel has spoken words that struck John with awe, but John now has the testimony of Jesus, and therefore he too can prophesy words capable of causing the future! These words stand before us today in which we too must share and amaze, but take care that we do not worship the wrong thing, not the messenger, not even the Bible itself. God alone and the Lamb do we worship! When we drop to knees in worship, we dare not aim our worship too low. Worship God, not the whore!

How Does It All End: Hell and Destruction?

The White Horse

Then I saw heaven opened, and there was a white horse! Its rider is called Faithful and True, and in righteousness he judges and makes war. His eyes are like a flame of fire, and on his head are many diadems; and he has a name inscribed that no one knows but himself. He is clothed in a robe dipped in blood, and his name is called The Word of God. And the armies of heaven, wearing fine linen, white and pure, were following him on white horses. From his mouth comes a sharp sword with which to strike down the nations, and he will rule them with a rod of iron; he will tread the wine press of the fury of the wrath of God the

> Almighty. On his robe and on his thigh he has a name inscribed, "King of kings and Lord of lords."
>
> Revelation 19:11-16 (NRSV)

The white horse finally appears again! He is called the Faithful and True, names belonging to Christ Jesus. There are two sides to his divinity; not only is he faithful and true, he also judges and punishes. His name is called the Word of God! Like I mentioned, this Word of God with a blood-soaked robe has been around since creation. The Word of God and the testimony of the Lamb are one in the same, and their message is rather simple—Trust God! Take care of this wonderful creation and love one another! Yet we have seen throughout the book we do not obey. Therefore, while it seems in these passages Christ is riding out for the last battle we must always remember Revelation is a story about the past, present, and future. It is not so much a vision about what Christ is going to do, but what Christ is doing.

Bedtime Stories

> Then I saw an angel standing in the sun, and with a loud voice he called to all the birds that fly in midheaven, "Come, gather for the great supper of God, to eat the flesh of kings, the flesh of captains, the flesh of the mighty, the flesh of horses and their riders, flesh of all, both free and slave, both small and great." Then I saw the beast and the kings of the earth with their armies gathered to make war against the rider on the horse and against his army. And the beast was captured, and

> with it the false prophet who had performed in its presence the signs by which he deceived those who had received the mark of the beast and those who worshiped its image. These two were thrown alive into the lake of fire that burns with sulfur. And the rest were killed by the sword of the rider on the horse, the sword that came from his mouth; and all the birds were gorged with their flesh.
>
> Revelation 19:17-21 (NRSV)

Not bedtime stories you want to read to your young ones? The birds of the air can expect a feast when God's war comes to an end. There is no question the end will come and also no question of the outcome the last battle already decided by God. I think we can all honestly admit that the beast from the sea, the beast from the earth, realities of evil will someday come to an end. Jesus tells us personally in Matthew 13:40 his angels/messengers will take "all causes of sin and all evildoers, and throw them into the furnace of fire." Yes, this day will happen. When? Your guess is as good as mine, but I have a sneaking suspicion it will not be in 2012!

The Binding of Satan

> Then I saw an angel coming down from heaven, holding in his hand the key to the bottomless pit and a great chain. He seized the dragon, that ancient serpent, who is the Devil and Satan, and bound him for a thousand years, and threw him into the pit, and locked and sealed it over him, so that he would deceive the nations no more, until

the thousand years were ended. After that he must be let out for a little while.

Revelation 20:1-3 (NRSV)

These few verses have caused much controversy. What is the meaning of Satan's thousand years of imprisonment? First of all, since we have found much relevant symbolism throughout this fascinating book, I think it would be wrong and rather silly to now simply assume that the one thousand years is a literal one thousand years, or the binding an actual binding with real keys and chains. I can't tell you how many interpretations I have found regarding this one short text. Most common, but wrong is that before the end of times there will be one thousand years on earth where evil will not prevail, sometimes referred to as the millennium kingdom. While this is a fond thought, it is not biblically sound. It's not even mentally sound. To find a solid meaning I think we must do what Revelation does and turn to the context of the rest of Scripture. Granted on the surface it sounds like the one thousand years of Satan's imprisonment has not yet arrived. All one needs to do is read the paper, watch the evening news to see that Satan is alive and well, living in our communities today. So naturally, one begins to think the passage talks about a future event. But is that the case? What does Scripture say? Scripture, believe it or not, says Satan has been bound! That's correct! Scripture teaches that evil has been tied up and chained with the first coming of Jesus the Christ.

The gospels of Matthew, Mark, and Luke all tell a story or parable of the strong man, fully armed who guards his own palace so that his goods are safe. In Matthew 12:29 and Mark 3:27 the texts are identical. They read, "How can one enter a strong man's house and plunder his property, without first tying up the strong man; then indeed the house can be plundered" (NRSV). In Luke 11:21-22 the text reads, "When a strong man, fully armed, guards his castle, his property is safe. But when one stronger than he attacks him and overpowers him, he takes away his armor in which he trusted and divides his plunder" (NRSV). In both cases we know from the context the stories are told to illustrate something happened to Satan and it happened at the incarnation or the birth of Christ Jesus. In Christ's first coming, the kingdom of God arrived on earth in a visible manner with Jesus entering the strong man's house and casting out evil spirits continually, demonstrating his power over the dragon. Satan for all his strength has been seized and bound!

While to us it may seem like evil has continued pretty much at liberty, there is no escaping the fact that in all the gospels Satan is bound. Not only bound, but at the birth of Christ, evil is also thrown into the pit in order that he should deceive the nations no more. Here again our first thought is to say this must reference the future because the nations are still being deceived, but again consider what is being said in the rest of Scripture. When Christ is born the aged Simeon in Luke 2:30 recognizes the baby he holds is the Messiah. Simeon lifts up his voice saying, "For my eyes have seen your salvation, which you have prepared in the presence of all peoples, a light for revelation to the Gentiles and for glory to your people Israel" (NRSV).

During the earthly life of Jesus, the undeceiving of the nations begins to take place. If you recall at Jesus's birth, he is visited by poor shepherds and wise men from far away lands. In his adult life, Jesus has dramatic contacts with a Roman centurion, a Canaanite woman, and a company of Greeks. Even after the death and resurrection of Christ and the formation of the church, people from every nation under heaven come together on the day of Pentecost and a blossoming of the gospel is begun by the conversion of people from Mesopotamia, Judea, Cappadocia, Pontus, Asia, Phrygia, Pamphylia, Egypt, Libya, and Rome. The gospel and deeds of God's power will be preached to all nations, and my dear friends, it is still being preached! One should say the one-thousand-year-binding of Satan is exactly the same number as the reign of the church. Since the church still exists today we are living in the three-and-a-half-years, the forty-two months, the 1260 days, and now the one thousand years in which Satan has been bound, simply presenting another beautiful picture with a number assigned for our benefit.

Let me ask you a question. What would the world be like if Satan were not bound by the gospel? What would it be like if terrorists, murderers, rapists, and drug dealers were not bound by bars? We know simply being locked up does not totally eliminate the work of these evil people, but it sure slows down the damage they may cause. In the same manner, the binding of Satan agrees with the gospels where Christ makes one of his top priorities that of casting out evil spirits and spreading this sharp two-edge-sword message to people of all nations, slowing down the damage the devil can accomplish here on earth. Also each and every time someone accepts this gospel message and is added to the church, the woman, the 144,000, the great multitude, Satan's inability to deceive the nations is proclaimed again and again and again; the thousand years of Satan being bound and imprisoned began with Christ's first coming and is still in progress.

Yet the text reminds us there will come a time when Satan will be freed from the restraints that the church or the bride has placed upon it, that of deceiving the nations. Therefore, Satan's thousand years of imprisonment will come to an end when the gospel ceases to be proclaimed! At this point we will logically experience this resurgence of evil rising up at the end of time, a time where the beast will turn against the whore, Satan will rise up against Satan, a divided house and there will be all out chaos and destruction. The ultimate battle will take place at the end of the so-called thousand years, and Satan will once again come out to deceive the nations in full force. Once the restraints are off, the world will again experience the full activity of Satan with all the wicked deception. However, the second coming of Christ will put an end once and for all to this final outbreak of evil.

THE THOUSAND-YEAR REIGN

> Then I saw thrones, and those seated on them were given authority to judge. I also saw the souls of those who had been beheaded for their testimony to Jesus and for the word of God. They had not worshiped the beast or its image and

had not received its mark on their foreheads or their hands. They came to life and reigned with Christ a thousand years. (The rest of the dead did not come to life until the thousand years were ended.) This is the first resurrection. Blessed and holy are those who share in the first resurrection. Over these the second death has no power, but they will be priests of God and of Christ, and they will reign with him a thousand years. When the thousand years are ended, Satan will be released from his prison and will come out to deceive the nations at the four corners of the earth, Gog and Magog, in order to gather them for battle; they are as numerous as the sands of the sea. They marched up over the breadth of the earth and surrounded the camp of the saints and the beloved city. And fire came down from heaven and consumed them. And the devil who had deceived them was thrown into the lake of fire and sulfur, where the beast and the false prophet were, and they will be tormented day and night forever and ever. Then I saw a great white throne and the one who sat on it; the earth and the heaven fled from his presence, and no place was found for them. And I saw the dead, great and small, standing before the throne, and books were opened. Also another book was opened, the book of life. And the dead were judged according to their works, as recorded in the books. And the sea gave up the dead that were in it, Death and Hades gave up the dead that were in them, and all were judged according to what they had done. Then Death and Hades were thrown into the lake of fire. This is the second death, the lake of fire; and anyone whose name was not found written in the book of life was thrown into the lake of fire.

Revelation 20:4-15 (NRSV)

I'm going out on a limb all by my lonesome because I disagree with about every single commentary regarding this short passage. Most of them talk about the first resurrection being a person's rebirth as a Christian. The second death they claim refers to the time of judgment. Yet, for the most part, I feel they are missing the mark in a mammoth way.

Since the one-thousand-year binding of Satan is now in progress and evil has been thrown into the pit through the first coming of Christ Jesus and through the birth of the Christian church, now all those who have not worshiped the beast or its image when they die the first death, these fortunate souls will reign with Christ until the second coming, the end times.

Let me put it another way. You do realize life on this planet is rather short? At some point in the near future, you will die! If you have been marked with the seal of God and have taken care of God's good creation, if you have accepted the forgiveness God has freely offered you through Christ and you have washed your robe in the blood of the Lamb, if you have trusted in God and not worshiped the institutions and its message, then you my friend have nothing to worry about! Your name is in the book of life! When you die the first death, God's promise is that you will come to life and live with Christ the remaining existence of creation! The second death or the final judgment will play no part in your life! Did you hear that? The second death or even the final judgment will play no part in your life!

However, and this is another big however, the ones who worshiped the beasts and the whore will never experience the first resurrection. The text itself tells us.

Yes, they will experience the first death like everyone else, but not the first resurrection. Instead those who die the first death and do not have their robes washed in the blood of the Lamb will simply rot in the ground, or doing whatever dead people do, waiting until the end times.

When the thousand years is up, when the gospel ceases to be proclaimed, Satan will be loosed, and the world will end shortly because there can only be one battle as universal and final as this one. It is the great day of wrath. It is Armageddon! It is the clash where the beasts gather with the kings of the earth and their armies to fight against the rider on the white horse. It is Gog and Magog, who simply happen to be another picture or symbol of the end times found in the Hebrew Scriptures. Ezekiel, a Hebrew prophet, talks about Gog (a person) and Magog (a territory) fighting against Israel sometime in the seventh century BCE. Whatever we desire to call it, the great day of wrath, Armageddon, or even Gog and Magog, after the thousand years has ended there will be a climatic battle in history and the end of world.

Revelation is now trying its hardest to convince us to make a choice before this time comes. There is only Christ and Satan! Christ who lives forever and those with him, or Satan who dies forever and those with him. Every single day of your life, you are choosing your fate. Will you experience the first resurrection? Because there will be a final judgment and there may well be a second death for some!

At the end of the world, the second coming, after rotting in the ground for however long the gospel is being proclaimed, the text tells us the dead will be raised from the ground and from the sea. The ones who put their faith in the beast and its message will graciously be given one last chance to plead their case. These it says will be judged by what they have done and only if their names are written in the book of life! Does this give those who have not repented and followed the Lamb one last chance? I don't know. This is up to Christ and whether that person's name is in the book of life! Do you really want to take that chance?

If one has not accepted the shame of sin and the glory of salvation earned by the slaughtered Lamb, then they have nothing to plead but their own works and goodness. How many of us are truly worthy? Anyone whose name is not found written in the book of life will be thrown into the lake of fire for eternity. Start now and pray that you will be part of that first resurrection! If this vision doesn't give you something to think about, nothing will.

IT IS DONE!

> Then I saw a new heaven and a new earth; for the first heaven and the first earth had passed away, and the sea was no more. And I saw the holy city, the new Jerusalem, coming down out of heaven from God, prepared as a bride adorned for her husband. And I heard a loud voice from the throne saying, "See, the home of God is among mortals. He will dwell with them; they will be his peoples, and God himself will be with them; he will wipe every tear from their eyes. Death will be no more; mourning and crying and pain will be

no more, for the first things have passed away." And the one who was seated on the throne said, "See, I am making all things new." Also he said, "Write this, for these words are trustworthy and true." Then he said to me, "It is done! I am the Alpha and the Omega, the beginning and the end. To the thirsty I will give water as a gift from the spring of the water of life. Those who conquer will inherit these things, and I will be their God and they will be my children. But as for the cowardly, the faithless, the polluted, the murderers, the fornicators, the sorcerers, the idolaters, and all liars, their place will be in the lake that burns with fire and sulfur, which is the second death."

Revelation 21:1-8 (NRSV)

I debated whether to place this section at the end of "Destruction and Hell," or the beginning of the next section "Salvation and Heaven." Yet isn't that true of life? Doesn't what we do in this brief earthly existence walk the fine line between that of heaven and hell? However, I decided to include it at the end of judgment because there will be one, judgment that is, and we need to think seriously about that judgment. According to the text, God will always be with those who follow the Lamb. Death will be no more; crying and pain will be no more. These words are trustworthy and true! If you are thirsty, if you desire to worship and praise God, you receive these fabulous gifts without payment. Throughout the book, over and over again the signs and warnings are given. Here however, those who do not worship the Lamb, who worship the beasts, will be placed in the lake that burns with fire and sulfur, which is the second death. There is no more hope. There are no more second chances. Over and out! Like the text says, "It is done!" How will it end for *you*?

How Does It All End: Salvation and Heaven?

Then one of the seven angels who had the seven bowls full of the seven last plagues came and said to me, "Come, I will show you the bride, the wife of the Lamb." And in the spirit he carried me away to a great, high mountain and showed me the holy city Jerusalem coming down out of heaven from God. It has the glory of God and a radiance like a very rare jewel, like jasper, clear as crystal. It has a great, high wall with twelve gates, and at the gates twelve angels, and on the gates are inscribed the names of the twelve tribes of the Israelites; on the east three gates, on the north three gates, on the south three gates, and on the west three gates. And the wall of the city has twelve foundations, and on them are the twelve names of the twelve apostles of the Lamb.

The angel who talked to me had a measuring rod of gold to measure the city and its gates and walls. The city lies foursquare, its length the same as its width; and he measured the city with his rod, fifteen hundred miles; its length and width and height are equal. He also measured its wall, one hundred forty-four cubits by human measurement, which the angel was using. The wall is built of jasper, while the city is pure gold, clear as glass. The foundations of the wall of the city are adorned with every jewel; the first was jasper, the second sapphire, the third agate, the fourth emerald, the fifth onyx, the sixth carnelian, the seventh chrysolite, the eighth beryl, the ninth topaz, the tenth chrysoprase, the eleventh jacinth, the twelfth amethyst. And the twelve gates are twelve pearls, each of the gates is a single pearl, and the street of the city is pure gold, transparent as glass. I saw no temple in the city, for its temple is the Lord God the Almighty and the Lamb. And the city has no need of sun or moon to shine on it, for the glory of God is its light, and its lamp is the Lamb. The nations will walk by its light, and the kings of the earth will bring their glory into it. Its gates will never be shut by day and there will be no night there. People will bring into it the glory and the honor of the nations. But nothing unclean will enter it, nor anyone who practices abomination or falsehood, but only those who are written in the Lamb's book of life.

Then the angel showed me the river of the water of life, bright as crystal, flowing from the throne of God and of the Lamb through the middle of the street of the city. On either side of the river is the tree of life with its twelve kinds of fruit, producing its fruit each month; and the leaves of the tree are for the healing of the nations. Nothing accursed will be found there any more. But the throne of God and of the Lamb will be in it, and his servants will worship him; they will see his face, and his name will be on their foreheads. And there will be no more night; they need no light of lamp or sun, for the Lord God will be their light, and they will reign forever and ever.

Revelation 21:9-22:5 (NRSV)

As always, there is a counterpart, an alternative in each and every scene of Revelation. Here the concept of the bride is reintroduced; the lampstands, the twenty-four elders, the inhabitants of heaven, the great multitude, the 144,000—in short the bride is all people of God in all ages. It is you! It is me! We have been wed to the Lamb, cleansed by his blood, and we are to remain faithful as a bride remains true to her mate, not like all the fornication of the whore. The bride is now worthy, not by earning it, but simply by association. The church, even unworthy, is now raised to a place of honor by her beloved Husband in the wedding feast of heaven!

No writer is capable of describing in more detail what heaven must be like than the writer of Revelation. The text says it all! John's vision shows the holy city of Jerusalem, its walls and gates, even its measurements with all its beauty. We see God giving this city light, light from a rare jewel. We see the gates and walls bearing the names of the twelve tribes and the twelve apostles. Its walls are precious stones, every gate a single pearl; the buildings and open spaces of the city made of inconceivable crystal clear gold declaring God's glory. The light of God's Spirit shines from within. It is clothed in a beauty we can barely imagine. There is no temple because to be in heaven is to be with God. God's glory invades every nook and cranny, even the gold is transparent. Its gates are open to all people, the Jews, the Gentiles, or simply everybody, all nations, all people regardless of race, wealth, brains, power, or influence. All that is truly good and beautiful in this world will reappear in heaven, purified and enhanced in the perfect setting as God intended. Nothing of real value we find on earth will be lost in heaven. The only thing that disqualifies a person from entering the presence of God is sin. The text says, "There will no more be anything accursed." The only thing that will qualify a person to enter is their name written in the book of life. These are two sides of the same coin. Either one is excluded from the presence of God or one trusts in the crucified Christ for the forgiveness of sin. If one does the latter, the Lord God will be their light and they shall reign forever and ever.

Conclusion

HE IS COMING SOON!

And he said to me, "These words are trustworthy and true, for the Lord, the God of the spirits of the prophets, has sent his angel to show his servants what must soon take place." See, I am coming soon! Blessed is the one who keeps the words of the prophecy of this book.

Revelation 22:6-7 (NRSV)

The beginning of Revelation and its ending are the same. Both are concerned about "what must soon take place." The real message of God is always concerned with what must soon take place. God's method in getting the message across has been through certain chosen people, supremely through Jesus. Before the three-

and-a-half years of Christ's ministry, it was the nation of Israel and the fellowship of the prophets, and after the glorious company of apostles who are God's messengers. The message they pass on through the Holy Scriptures represent words that are trustworthy and true, which God passes on with the Holy Spirit to the hearts and minds of humans, to you. Now it is you who must take these words that are trustworthy and true and convey them to others. Because it concerns "what must soon take place."

In seminary, I had a professor by the name of Pete Pero. He said something I will never forget. Pete said, "There are only two options when it comes to the validity of the Holy Scriptures. The Word is either true or it is not true. Simply put, if they are not true when you die, none of it will matter a hill of beans, none of it! However, and this is a big however, if the Word found here is true, then it must have tremendous meaning not only in my life today, but for all eternity." Pete paused for a moment and continued. "Don't you think with the stakes so high and only two options available, one would at least invest the time and effort to read and ponder these words of knowledge that are either true or not true?"

The knowledge of God that comes to us through the prophecy of this book and by the Bible as a whole cannot help but bring a blessing, and the blessing is a better understanding of God and our purpose. The attentive obedient study of Scripture produces not a mind stuffed with knowledge, but a spirit awakened into true life. So yes, as the text reminds us, blessed are those who read aloud these words and keep them! The

Word of God in this book as we are told in its opening verses is a Revelation given by God to Christ, by Christ to the angel, by the angel to John, and by John to you, without at any stage losing its divine authority, so what John writes is what God has said, and one must admit God has taught us a great deal in this one-of-a-kind piece of literature.

God has shown every church throughout the world his love and compassion by offering encouragement and advice in order that Christ, bearing the gospel of love and forgiveness may remain in the center of each lampstand. God has given us a glimpse of the heavenly throne and those around it, whose purpose is to sing songs of praise and worship, not only to the One seated upon the throne, but also to the slaughtered Lamb, who just happens to be the only one capable of explaining our past, our present, and our future. It is a history riddled with war and terrorism, economic injustice leading to death because of our reluctance to accept the everlasting gospel, a gospel pleading that we trust God and take care of this glorious creation, including each other.

Instead of relying upon the kingdom of God and the gospel of Christ, we place our trust in worldly institutions and their messages, creating a system of evil that grows and gains power as time moves on. We are painted a clear picture of these beasts and whores and what lies in store for them. We see and hear the warnings all trying so desperately to get our attention, because in the end, there will be a time of judgment. Some will spend eternity in heaven, others in hell. Who do you worship?

Who Do You Worship?

> I, John, am the one who heard and saw these things. And when I heard and saw them, I fell down to worship at the feet of the angel who showed them to me; but he said to me, "You must not do that! I am a fellow servant with you and your comrades the prophets, and with those who keep the words of this book. Worship God!" And he said to me, "Do not seal up the words of the prophecy of this book, for the time is near. Let the evildoer still do evil, and the filthy still be filthy, and the righteous still do right, and the holy still be holy. See, I am coming soon; my reward is with me, to repay according to everyone's work. I am the Alpha and the Omega, the first and the last, the beginning and the end." Blessed are those who wash their robes, so that they will have the right to the tree of life and may enter the city by the gates. Outside are the dogs and sorcerers and fornicators and murderers and idolaters, and everyone who loves and practices falsehood.
>
> Revelation 22:8-15 (NRSV)

Yet always remember when we worship, do not dare aim our sights too low. Worship God, not the dragon! Worship the Lamb, not the whore! The inspired Word of God has been given to you. What are you going to do with it? Do evil, be filthy, or do right and be holy? The end times will come, and it will be brought about by Christ, the beginning and end. It may not be tomorrow, it may not be 2012, it may not be 3099, but it will end when the gospel ceases to be proclaimed in word and action, and even then it will still be sooner than we would like. We must start now taking seriously the opportunities presented in this book to bring about change. We have the Hebrew Scriptures. We have the words of the prophets. We have the words of the apostles. Has your robe been washed in the blood of the Lamb? If not, the book makes clear who will be left outside and who will be allowed inside with access to the tree of life, once forbidden to Adam and Eve, now available to you and me.

The Warning Label and the End

> It is I, Jesus, who sent my angel to you with this testimony for the churches. I am the root and the descendant of David, the bright morning star. The Spirit and the bride say, "Come." And let everyone who hears say, "Come." And let everyone who is thirsty come. Let anyone who wishes take the water of life as a gift. I warn everyone who hears the words of the prophecy of this book: if anyone adds to them, God will add to that person the plagues described in this book; if anyone takes away from the words of the book of this prophecy, God will take away that person's share in the tree of life and in the holy city, which are described in this book. The one who testifies to these things says, "Surely I am coming soon." Amen. Come, Lord Jesus! The grace of the Lord Jesus be with all the saints. Amen.
>
> Revelation 22:16-21 (NRSV)

Finally, not only is there a blessing coming with the prayerful study of Revelation, the book closes with a warning label. If for some reason you feel what is found in John's vision is not enough to be saved, or you believe maybe you can get by without observing the commands of God, then I simply say, "The Lord be with you!" It all goes back to wanting God's knowledge, saying we know better than God. We do not! The closing is a serious warning for all who interpret Scripture to suit there own needs.

The book ends with Jesus reminding us once again that he is coming soon. There is only one thing we must do for the promises of God to bring a blessing in our lives, and that is to pray the earliest known prayer of the church, "Come, Lord Jesus. Come into our daily lives, and soon, today, this very hour! The grace of the Lord Jesus be with all the saints. Amen."